Custom Designed Reflection Guide

Ordinary People
Hearing God's Call

Wendy A.W. Berthelsen

Assisted by
Steven A. Harr

Dedicated to

Steve and Kathy Harr

for their
Generosity
and
Vision

for mobilizing
Ordinary People
"Called Out"
by
Jesus

TABLE OF CONTENTS

HOW TO GET THE MOST OUT OF THIS GUIDE

What to Expect!

Be the unique "you" the living God created, and is calling you to be! This is our hope and prayer! What follows is an integrated, practical, and interactive process to meaningfully seek the Lord and discover His call—what He is saying and doing in your everyday life—past, present and future. It is for ordinary people who want their entire life to have a real and transformative influence and impact on the world. This "call" journey is gathered around five parts, each with one or more chapters:

- The Power: The Holy Spirit in You!
- The Places: Your Unique Mission Field!
- The Plan: God and Ordinary People like You!
- The Purpose: Transform the World … Your Unique Part!
- Press On to Win the Race!

Each chapter may be engaged alone or in any order. Each may be reengaged over and over as God's dynamic call shifts and changes throughout your life. We assume that you label yourself a Christian or follower of Jesus. If you are unsure about these labels, still consider pursuing this journey. We believe you will find a deep and profound goodness.

Intentionally Invite God to Guide and Speak!

Invite the living God to guide you! Pay attention to your thoughts. The Holy Spirit will speak, using your inner promptings. Significant thoughts and strong impressions will come in no particular order and at no pre-planned time. Jesus will call whenever and however He desires; therefore, none of what follows is a program, recipe, easy formula or rigid steps. Rather it is an integrated journey, combining Scripture, teaching, exercises, prayerful reflection, inventories, conversation, prayers, and journaling. Parts of the journey are labeled "challenges." Though they may not appear easy, try them because they will likely unlock something significant. Write your reflections rather than just reading. Read each section in its entirety. Not everything may appear useful right now; however at another time, what was seemingly useless may be just what you need. Seek out trustworthy people to support you on this journey (see Chapter 7). Scripture, the Lord's living active word is throughout. Invite Jesus to call you through these life-giving words. Contemplate them. Memorize them, and they will always be a part of you, encouraging, speaking and calling! It is not by chance that the Hebrew word for the Hebrew Bible (recorded in the Old Testament) can be translated "calling."

Take Your Time!

You will not complete this process in a few hours or even a few days. However throughout, Jesus will be with you, leading and guiding. If you feel stumped, take a break. Make a date to return at another time. Reflect, pray, wait, and finally walk ahead!

For More Help, Consult the Companion Volume!

Each of the corresponding chapters in the companion volume, ***Custom Designed: A Life Worthy of the Call*** has more teaching, real life illustrations and scriptural insights.

INTRODUCTION

ORDINARY PEOPLE
HEARING GOD'S CALL

....

The Lord is Calling: 1 Corinthians 1:26-31; Jeremiah 1:4-10; Luke 1:26-38; Luke 2:21-40; Ephesians 1:17-23; 3:20-4:1; Matthew 13:31-33

Yes, Jesus is calling you! Miraculously all throughout history, the Lord has called ordinary people to transform and heal a broken world. It's God's ingenious plan. "Do not be afraid." The Lord has spoken these words over and over to ordinary people. Take them to heart.

Jesus has called ordinary men and women who were afraid and insecure, wayward and weak, wealthy and poor, young and old. The Lord equipped them with the power of His Spirit and all else needed to accomplish His call. Today the Son of God, Jesus still continues to call and equip ordinary people who may seem "small" in some way to have a "big" kingdom impact. In fact, Jesus said that God's kingdom is like the "smallest" seed that grows into the "biggest" garden tree, providing shelter for the birds (Matthew 13:31-32). Though you may feel "small" in some way, you're called to have a "big" kingdom impact, speaking and demonstrating the Lord's will and ways in order to transform people, places and problems.

Wherever you are today, we are praying to the Lord for you … for fresh vision, practical guidance, increased optimism, greater hope, less fear, more confidence, wise perspective, needed healing, miraculous power and new expectancy on this ever changing journey we call life. Jesus is able to deliver all that is needed in a powerful and creative way that human efforts alone cannot. So, do you know Jesus and His call?

Let's correct some misunderstandings! The Lord does not call just people in the Bible or pastors or missionaries or professional church workers. Rather Jesus is calling everyone, and more specifically and importantly He is calling you! Nor do these words mean that you will eventually become a professional church worker or foreign missionary. Nor are these "professionals" and their calls more important than your own significant part. All of these "professionals" are ordinary people just like you.

Perhaps you have never applied the word "call" to yourself. Instead you may have asked life-defining questions like: "What am I supposed to do?" or "Who am I?" These are familiar questions that we ask many times throughout our lives. Whether you use the word "call" or not, whether you believe in God or not, these life-defining questions are symptomatic of someone who is seeking and searching for the Lord's call. Jesus' call intersects with both your "being" and "doing," and knowing His call will likely provide some answers for these questions.

The apostle Paul wrote to ordinary everyday Christians of his time: "I am earnestly calling you to walk in conformity with the calling to which you were called." (Ephesians 4:1, Author's translation) Paul is saying, already the Lord has called you, now get to it … walk, act and live in a way that matches with the incredible worth and weightiness of this calling that you have been given. Since Jesus is calling and we all have a call, can there be anything in your life more important than for you to hear, answer, and know the fullness of His call? This alone is reason enough to seek and know His call. It is essential to be who the Lord Jesus desires for you to be.

Do you live in conformity with Jesus and His call? Can you recognize His personal and practical voice? Yes, Jesus is still speaking to His children, and desires to speak to you. Can you pinpoint what distracts and detours you from living worthy of Jesus and His call?

Together, we will seek Jesus and listen for His call, identifying what is needed to live worthy of His call. Already the Lord has empowered and equipped you for His call. He has prepared the places where He desires for you to carry out His call. Continually, Jesus is personally calling you to uniquely participate in His masterful plan and purposes—today, tomorrow and the next day. Jesus' call is dynamic, like journeying down a road. Where you are tomorrow will differ from today yet still connect with what is behind. To guide us on this journey, we will use five "P" words: power, places, plan, purpose, and press on … that is Jesus' power, His places, His plan, His purposes … and pressing on in the call to which He is calling you! Let's introduce those "P" words!

The POWER: Do you want your life to have a compelling and trans- formative impact and influence? You will need divine "power." Can you describe how God the Father and Creator has custom designed and empowered you for His call? In your mother's womb, from your first "breath" and when the Holy Spirit "breathed" His life and power into you, God has uniquely created, prepared and gifted you for all that He is calling you to do!

The PLACES: Where is Jesus calling you? Can you "incorporate" the Lord's call into all the "places" of your life? Though you may not travel across the ocean, you are called to be a missionary and you have a mission field. Mission comes from the Latin, misseo, meaning "send." Every day, Jesus calls and "sends" you "out" into the unique mission field of your life: home, work, community, world, and the gathering of believers that you call "church."

The PLAN: Do you know that you are an important person in Jesus' "plan"? The living God personally partners with human flesh, reaching out, inviting relationship and calling for participation in His purposes … this is His "plan!" The Word made flesh—Jesus, God's Son most clearly proclaimed and demonstrated the Father's plan and purposes, and is still calling, teaching and training ordinary people including you for the Father's plan and purposes.

The PURPOSE: Do you know your unique part in Jesus' ongoing transformative intentions for the world? Jesus demonstrated the great reversal of sin, death, evil and the power of the devil. He brought God's loving and healing presence and power. Jesus proclaimed God's heavenly rule and reign, recreating, reforming and renewing people, places and problems. And so can you! Jesus is calling!

PRESS ON! Do you feel as if you are forever distracted and detoured from what is most important, especially life with the living God? "Press on" is race language from the Scriptures. You are encouraged to pursue Jesus' call as if you wanted to win an Olympic race. So what makes an Olympic racer successful? Much of the same will make you effective in "running the race"—living worthy of Jesus and His call.

It may surprise you, but pure and simple, this is real church. Maybe you are disillusioned or dislike "church." That's okay. I get disillusioned also. For a moment, let's rethink "church." Church in the Biblical Greek literally means "called out ones." Church is ordinary people "called out" by Jesus. You are the church. Church is not a place, building, institution or organization. Church is not an end in itself. Rather, it is you, me and all other Christians "called out" by Jesus to transform the world … in our families, work, communities, world and also in the gathering of Christians that we label "church" (Yes, we still need to gather together with other followers of Jesus). We the "Christian church"—you and I—will only be able to fulfill God's will if we pursue the identity given in our name, the "called out ones." What sense does it make for you and me—the church, the "called out ones"—to not seek and know the Lord's call? To do so is to miss the very heart of what "church" is about. Sadly this misunderstanding causes many gatherings of Jesus' followers labeled "church" to fall short. It is time to turn this around!

We are resurrection people. What difference does this make? It makes all the difference in the world because if there was no resurrection, then Jesus could not be alive in your life. You see, Jesus is still alive in this earthly existence and He desires to be alive in your life … is He? Jesus is still reaching out, relating to ordinary people like you … do you know Him? Jesus is still present, personally partnering with human flesh, calling people like you … are you partnering with Him? Jesus still desires to reform, recreate and renew all of His creation including your life and living … is He? Jesus is still communicating and calling … even you … can you hear Him? Let's press on!

"May the God of peace, who through the blood of the eternal covenant brought back from the dead our Lord Jesus, that great Shepherd of the sheep, equip you with everything good for doing his will, and may he work in us what is pleasing to him, through Jesus Christ, to whom be glory forever and ever. Amen." Hebrews 13:20-21

First Challenge: Find Some Time

You will need to find some time to seek Jesus' life-giving call. Where do you waste time or use it on the insignificant? For most people, a little less TV or internet would create time. Reflect upon the rhythm of your week. You may have several smaller spaces of time or one larger one. Ask the Lord to show you when, where, and how you will navigate this journey of seeking His call. Make a date with the Lord and yourself. Write spaces of time that might work for you. How will you protect this time?

_____

_____

_____

Reflect upon these living active words:

"Be careful then how you live, not as unwise people but as wise, making the most of the time, because the days are evil. So do not be foolish but understand what the will of the Lord is." Ephesians 5:15-17 NRSV

Second Challenge: Where do you need to start?

Reflect upon the five "P" words: "power," "place," "plan," "purpose," and "pressing on." Which grabs your attention or perks your interest? Which is the greatest mystery? Which is most needed? Record your thoughts.

_____

_____

_____

Slowly and prayerfully, hear the Lord speak through His word. What is He saying to you?

"For surely I know the plans I have for you, says the LORD, plans for your welfare and not for harm, to give you a future with hope." Jeremiah 29:11 NRSV

Third Challenge: Call?

When you hear the word "call," what immediately comes to mind? How do you feel?

_____

_____

_____

"God is calling you." What immediately comes to mind? How do you feel?

_____

_____

_____

Describe how the living God is presently involved in your life.

_____

_____

_____

After recording your answer, reflect upon the Lord's words spoken to you:

"Now the word of the LORD came to me saying, 'Before I formed you in the womb I knew you, and before you were born I consecrated you; I appointed you...'" Jeremiah 1:4-5 NRSV

Fourth Challenge: Inventory Your Concerns and Fears

What concerns do you have? What fears do you have? What do you most fear? Begin to identify your concerns and fears.

_____

_____

_____

Identifying and confronting your concerns and fears can diminish them, taking away their paralyzing effect. Surrender them to the Lord. Ask the Lord to reveal what is causing the fear. Continue to inventory any new concerns or fears. Jesus is speaking these words to you:

"Peace I leave with you; my peace I give to you. I do not give to you as the world gives. Do not let your hearts be troubled, and do not be afraid." John 14:27

Prayer: Loving God, speak to me through your powerful Word. Guide me. Inspire my thoughts, desires and emotions. Take away my fears. I surrender my fears to you. Give me inner courage. Lead and guide me. Thank you for custom designing and creating me. Call me. You have unique and important work for me to do. Fill my entire life with your joy and peace. In Jesus' name, Amen

Further Thoughts and Actions:

- **For more insight and real life illustrations,** study the introduction in the companion volume, *Custom Designed: A Life Worthy of the Call.*

- **Continue to inventory your concerns and fears.**

- **Random Thoughts:** Record any thoughts, feelings, ideas or actions that come to you.

CHAPTER 1
GOD IS CALLING YOU!

The Lord is Calling: Luke 14:16-20; Matthew 25:14-30; Mark 4:1-20; Psalm 27; Exodus 3:1-4:17; Jonah

In order to run the race and reach the finish line, knowing your departure point is important as well as the detours and distractions along the way. So, where are you today?

Seeking significance or something new? Discouraged and disillusioned? Is the grass greener on the other side of the fence? Contemplating a crossroads? Fighting feelings of failure? Tarrying too long on a tangent or in transition? Buried beneath a burden? Distracted by many demands? Does any of this characterize you?

Who am I? What should I do? Where am I going? Are you asking life-defining questions? Do the answers seem hard to find? Perhaps, your life may have taken a significant turn, for better or so it seems, for worse. Therefore, you want in earnest to know who you are and what it is you are supposed to be doing.

Jesus told parables. Parables are stories or allegories about God, real life, real people and more importantly about you. Jesus told parables about His call. Once He said:

"A certain man was preparing a great banquet and "called" many guests. At the time of the banquet he sent his servant to tell those who had been called, 'Come, for everything is now ready.' But they all alike began to make excuses. The first said, 'I have just bought a field, and I must go and see it. Please excuse me.' Another said, 'I have just bought five yoke of oxen, and I'm on my way to try them out. Please excuse me.' Still another said, 'I just got married, so I can't come.'" Luke 14:16-20 Author's translation

Clearly Jesus' call is like an invitation to a great banquet. The banquet is not just about a destination called heaven, but it is also about fullness of life right now! Yet many decline the invitation because they have other seemingly more important things to do. Wouldn't it be tragic to live life and miss out on what God has in mind for your life? So how about you? Jesus is calling you to a "great banquet." Will you show up? Why or why not? Check all the hurdles that currently apply to you:

_____ You simply have never thought about the Lord's call.

_____ You may be stretched or even exhausted, spending all your time trying to attack what seemingly needs to be done each day.

_____ You spend your time trying to survive day by day.

_____ Other things seem more important than God's call.

_____ What is most practical drives your decisions.

_____ Jesus' call might lead to change, suggesting that presently your life is falling short or some kind of failure.

_____ Your life is driven by the expectations of others. You are afraid of what others might think if you pursued something different from their expectations.

_____ You are afraid that others will think poorly of you if you were to follow Jesus and His call.

_____ You are afraid of what the Lord might expect of you.

_____ You are caught up in attaining "success" as measured by yourself or those around you.

_____ You are thinking about the missing piece on your resume.

_____ You are adept at many things, and maybe you have never invested the time to ask what the Lord might desire for your gifts and talents, or what you would actually enjoy (bring inner joy).

_____ You are convinced that it is not possible to have inner joy in your life.

Do you see yourself in any of these mental hurdles? I urge you to find a way to neutralize and minimize these hurdles. Because of them, perhaps your life is not driven by Jesus' call.

Many of these hurdles have at their core something familiar to all of us ... fear. Though some fear is helpful, warning us of danger, there is also fear that hinders, detours and even paralyzes. Fear of this type is one of the devil's weapons to distract and destroy God's children.

Perhaps a couple of insights may be helpful to you. First you are not alone in your fears and concerns. The Lord already knows all of them. Your concerns are real, shared by others and can be a helpful signal. They can help you to meaningfully address and confront whatever is behind them, perhaps a need for healing from something hurtful. When I shared my fear of a particular situation with an early coach in my life, he told me, _"If you were not concerned, I wouldn't have you on my team."_ Essentially, he told me that my concern meant that I cared and was motivated to address the concern rather than run from it. How about you?

Second I want you to firmly know that Jesus your Lord and Savior is not the author or source of fear. Because the Lord understands how easily we become afraid, over and over, Jesus speaks to us: *"Do not be afraid."* In fact, these words are the most common words found in Scripture. Jesus is reminding us that with Him, there is no reason to fear. More than you can imagine, Jesus wants you to know exactly who you are, why you are here and what you are to do. He wants you to hear His call. As a result, He will be with you every single step, speaking and guiding.

Observe and study Diagram A. Note those life-defining questions: "Who am I?" and "What am I to do?" We will return to this diagram several times as we explore those "P" words: power, places, plan, purpose and pressing on.

Let's consider the truth! God has called. God is calling. God will call. God calls. "Call" as we are speaking of it is not a noun; rather, it is a verb, and the subject of that verb is the living God, Father Son and Holy Spirit. God is the Caller. Wherever you find yourself right now, God who is the Caller is calling you. The almighty and all powerful God desires to partner with you, giving you all that is required. You see, the God who calls ordinary people is a BIG God who has created the universe, all time, all space, and knows each little detail of it all, including every detail about you. This God is already and always present and active in the world in spite of you and me. Even when we are totally wrapped up in the concerns and worries of life and not paying the least bit of attention to the God of the universe, He is lovingly at work. Has this truth sunk deep into your heart and set you free? This is what we are hoping and praying. So, let's press on!

Jesus is Calling!

Know Follow Serve

Who am I?

Interests Dreams Spiritual Creativity Personality
Passions Gifts

Knowledge Burdens
For the
World

Talents
Abilities
Skills Resources

Experience Listening & Seeking
God's Guidance Identity

Listening to God's WORD

Listening to Trustworthy Companions

What Am I to Do?

Where?

Family Work

Church

World

Diagram A

"Now to him who is able to do immeasurably more than all we ask or imagine, according to his power that is at work within us, to him be glory in the church and in Christ Jesus throughout all generations, forever and ever!" Ephesians 3:20-21

First Challenge: What is Happening Right Now?

What is happening in your life? Where do you feel content? What causes restlessness or concern? What feels confusing or "foggy?" Where are you searching? Write some words to characterize your life's condition right now.

_____

_____

_____

Maybe you are navigating a significant life-changing event. Are you going through one of these transitions? All of these are a bit like acts of a play as the plot of your life unfolds. Circle those that apply to you:

- Finishing High School
- In College
- Anticipating the Work Force
- Newly Married
- Anticipating Children
- Changing Jobs
- Empty Nest
- 40 Something and Restless
- Anticipating Retirement
- Retired... but not as you hoped
- Life-changing Experiences: divorce, loss of job, death, major health issues, addiction recovery, disillusionment, depression, despair

How do you feel? Perhaps one or more of these words describe your feelings: lost, optimistic, hopeful, encouraged, restless, anxious, worried, discontent, unsettled, discouraged, empty, afraid, guilty, grieving, confused, bored or hurting. Remember human emotions are normal and important clues. Describe your feelings right now. Try to identify what is driving them. Ask yourself: *"Why do I feel this way? What am I afraid of?"*

_____

_____

_____

Picture and know that Jesus is with you right now, speaking to you:

"Cast all your anxiety on him, because he cares for you." 1 Peter 5:7 NRSV

Second Challenge: Minimize Your Mental Hurdles

Reconsider the checklist of mental hurdles found above. What is it that has prevented you from freely and seriously seeking the Lord and His call? Is your response on the checklist, or is it something else?

_____

_____

_____

Here is a challenge. Now go to someone who you completely trust... someone who will take you seriously, knows you well and likely loves you. Show them the checklist of hurdles. Ask them to identify the hurdles that they believe apply to you. Ask for helpful suggestions on how to neutralize your hurdles. If you are puzzled on who to ask, read Chapter 7.

_____

_____

_____

Did you learn anything new? Maybe you did, or maybe not. Why or why not? Would you seek this person's counsel again? Why or why not? If this person wasn't helpful, try someone else.

_____

_____

_____

Sit for a moment in silence. Pray to the Lord. Ask Him to reveal a strategy for neutralizing your hurdles. Who could help you? Record your thoughts.

_____

_____

_____

Continue to seek insight related to your mental hurdles. Pray these words of promise:

"The Lord will fulfill his purpose for me; your steadfast love, O LORD, endures forever. Do not forsake the work of your hands." Psalm 138:8 NRSV

Third Challenge: Who am I? and What am I to do?

"Who am I?" "What am I to do?" "How and where do I find the answers?" Right now, how would you answer each of these significant questions?

_____

_____

_____

"Who am I?" "What am I to do?" "How and where do I find the answers?" Again, study Diagram A. What is most puzzling about these questions and diagram? What is most exciting?

_____

_____

_____

Be patient and have a long-term view! This journey will take time and effort, but it will be well worth it. Remember Jesus is already present and active in your life. He promises to be with you always. Today tomorrow and the next day, Jesus is calling you!

"I will instruct you and teach you the way you should go; I will counsel you with my eye upon you. Do not be like a horse or a mule, without understanding, whose temper must be curbed with bit and bridle, else it will not stay near you." Psalm 32:8-9 NRSV

Prayer: Now to you O Lord who is able to do immeasurably more than all I ask or imagine, according to your power that is at work within me, to you be glory in my life along with all of the "called out ones" and in Christ Jesus throughout all generations, forever and ever! Enable me to walk in conformity with the calling to which you have called me. Amen (Based upon Ephesians 3:20-4:1)

Further Thoughts and Actions

- Study the companion volume, *Custom Designed: A Life Worthy of the Call.* For real life illustrations and to develop added insight, examine the corresponding chapter.

- **Who do you deeply trust and respect?** Begin identifying people who might support and encourage you as you seek and pursue the Lord's call. For help, consult Chapter 7.

- **Keep a journal.** Writing can be a helpful, bringing greater clarity to you. Write when it works for you, even if very sporadically. Record your impressions, ideas, fears and all that God reveals to you. Use freedom and do not make this into a hard exercise.

- **Continue to inventory your concerns and fears.**

- **Random Thoughts:** Record any thoughts, feelings, ideas or actions that come to you.

THE POWER

THE HOLY SPIRIT IN YOU!

You will not be able to accomplish much of eternal significance without the Holy Spirit and His power. If you are a "Christian," already the living God has equipped and empowered you for what He is calling you to do! Thankfully, residing in you is the same power that created the world and raised Jesus from the dead. Wow! Contemplate that!

In the Old Testament, the living God called ordinary people to bring His kingdom rule and reign to a broken world. Oftentimes these "called" people were "anointed" with oil while the Lord simultaneously "anointed" them with His Spirit and power so that they could accomplish His call. Jesus also was "anointed" with the Spirit and power at his baptism:

"After being baptized, Jesus came up immediately from the water; and behold, the heavens were opened, and he saw the Spirit of God descending as a dove and lighting on Him, and behold, a voice out of the heavens said, 'This is My beloved Son, in whom I am well-pleased.'" Matthew 3:16-17 NASB

When Jesus was baptized and the Spirit descended upon Him, God the Father affirmed Jesus' identity: "Beloved Son" and the "Anointed One." "Messiah" in Biblical Hebrew and "Christ" in Biblical Greek literally mean "Anointed One." As a man, Jesus would not have been able to fulfill the Father's purposes and call without the "anointing," presence and power of the Holy Spirit. How much more is this true for us?

God, the Father and Creator intricately knit you together in your mother's womb. He already knew the days of your life. When you were born,

God breathed into you His breath, the spirit of life. You became a unique child, fearfully and wonderfully made. When you were born again from above and baptized, God again breathed into you His powerful Holy Spirit. You became a temple of the Holy Spirit. You were given His amazing and miraculous power and gifts. Like Jesus, the Spirit "anointed" you and the Father affirmed your identity, a "beloved child of God" and a "Christian." Like "Christ," "Christian" in Biblical Greek literally means "anointed one."

As a child of God, you are not a clone of another. Rather you have unique gifts, talents, experience and much more. To God, every detail about you is important. The Lord takes your unique individuality very seriously and you should also. Actually how God has created, empowered and prepared you will provide important clues and even point the way to what Jesus is calling you to be and do. Because you are custom designed by the Father, what the Lord is calling you to do is also unique and custom designed for you. Miraculously the Lord has uniquely crafted and gifted you for all that He is calling you to do!

Continually invite the Holy Spirit to fill you. Your gifts, attributes and all of who you are can be ignited with the Lord's boundless divine power, and then the possibilities of what God will do through you—an ordinary person— will be extraordinary.

The Power

Explore your identity as a child of God! Examine how you are uniquely "anointed" with His Spirit and power.

Chapter 2 Custom Designed and Called to Be a Unique Child of God
Chapter 3 Called to Be Empowered and Gifted

CHAPTER 2
CUSTOM DESIGNED AND CALLED TO BE A UNIQUE CHILD OF GOD

The Lord is Calling: Genesis 1:26-28, 2:7; Psalm 139; Isaiah 64:8; Ephesians 2:10; Romans 8:28

You are an amazing and marvelous creation of God. King David knew this and praised the Creator for how he was custom designed:

> *"For it was you who formed my inward parts; you knit me together in my mother's womb. I praise you, for I am fearfully and wonderfully made. Wonderful are your works; that I know very well. My frame was not hidden from you, when I was being made in secret, intricately woven in the depths of the earth." Psalm 139:13-14 NRSV*

Reflecting upon your custom design should move you to praise as well. Just consider your face. Your face is amazing in itself, and it most readily identifies you. All faces have two eyes, a nose, a mouth, two ears, skin, and all of this is supported and shaped by a bone structure. Though these attributes are limited, no two faces are exactly the same. Each of these attributes and their relationship with one another form your unique facial profile.

Reflect on Diagram A (see Chapter 1) once again. Under the question "Who am I?" you will note several attributes. Similar to your facial features, these attributes and their relationship with one another create a unique "profile" of you. Like a resumé, they characterize significant assets of your individuality. The Creator has custom designed you. By inventorying your unique attributes, you will uncover how the living God has already prepared you for His call. So, let's press on!

"Yet you, Lord, are our Father. We are the clay, you are the potter; we are all the work of your hand." Isaiah 64:8

First Challenge: Inventory Your Experience

To develop your unique "profile," relive your personal history. Contemplate both positive and negative experience from these arenas of your life: work, family, friends, neighborhood, community, world and the gathering of believers you call "church." Both positive and negative experiences have significantly shaped your individuality. If a negative experience was painful, God may have given you valuable insight and wisdom as a result of persevering through this experience. The insight that you gleaned might assist others in finding healing and wholeness.

Jot down experiences from your history. What has been meaningful or enjoyable? What has been the opposite? What has been difficult or painful? Invite the Lord to reveal experiences throughout your life. Be specific. For example for "Work," list all of your jobs since you were young. Consider which jobs were enjoyable and which were boring or discouraging.

Work:_____

_____

_____

Family: _____

_____

_____

Neighborhood/Community/World: _____

_____

_____

Church:_____

_____

_____

"And we know that in all things God works for the good of those who love him, who have been called according to his purpose." Romans 8:28

Second Challenge: Develop Your Unique Profile

Let's continue inventorying your attributes. This will be valuable and fulfilling.

Talents are aptitudes or gifts, given to you when you were born. For example, you may be musically talented or adept with numbers. **Skills and Abilities** are acquired through classes, seminars, experience or a mentor. Go to the checklist in Appendix A. It will help to identify your talents, skills and abilities. What aptitudes do others point out in you? Think about this as well. Record your seven to ten greatest talents, skills and abilities.

_____

_____

_____

Knowledge is learned information, expertise or wisdom gathered from a classroom, workshop, seminar, life experience, a significant mentor, hands-on learning, reading or research. This knowledge may be practical, related to a field of study or insight related to life: family, relationships or health. There is also spiritual or Biblical knowledge. Contemplate important formal and informal education experiences. Describe notable knowledge that you possess.

_____

_____

_____

Dreams and Passions: Close your eyes and retreat to your dreams. Dreams can become reality. Envision yourself doing something that meaningfully makes a difference or where you are driven, significantly motivated and lose all sense of time. What would this look like? When have you already experienced this? If you have, what caused it to be meaningful or motivating? Chapter 8 will assist in identifying dreams and passions.

_____

_____

_____

Interests and Hobbies: God is interested in your leisure and relaxation activities, and may call you to meaningfully use them. What are your interests and hobbies?

_____

_____

_____

Creativity: God has created you in His image; therefore you are creative. If you don't engage in artistic endeavors such as music, poetry or drama, you may think that you aren't creative. You may need to uncover your creative edge. Perhaps you are a creative thinker, problem solver, gift giver, homemaker or parent.

_____

_____

_____

Burdens for the World: God pours His love into your heart, causing it to ache with His compassion. You may be bearing a burden for the hungry, poor or lost. You may be concerned for the handicapped, imprisoned or those with AIDS. Perhaps you long for people to know significance or have passionate faith. You may be bothered by ineffective people, churches or government. You notice the need for justice, morality and truth. What causes you to lie awake at night? How could you attack these concerns? Chapter 8 will assist in uncovering your burdens for the world.

_____

_____

_____

Personality: Let's identify some of your personality preferences. All preferences have both advantages and disadvantages; so no particular set of preferences is ideal. People with varying preferences are needed, creating a beneficial balance. Knowing your preferences will allow you to work more effectively with others, both compensating for your weaknesses and valuing rather than critiquing others' differences. At some point, you may want to learn more about your personality by taking a Myers-Briggs Type Indicator. Circle your preferences from the following pairs. Keep in mind that even though you may be able to function quite well within either of them, usually you will have a preference one way or the other.

Task oriented ... People oriented

Structure ... Flexible

Planner ... Spontaneity

Big Picture ... Details

Intuitive ... Sensory

Hard Worker ... Rest and Play

Energized by being Alone ... Energized by being with Other People

Be in charge ... Have someone tell you what to do

With what age groups do you enjoy working? Do you like to work with a small group, large group, or work alone?

_____

_____

_____

Resources: Generous giving in order to make something happen can be very fulfilling. This may be why God has given you some of your resources. How could God use your home or other tangible things? For some, the mere mention of "giving" can cause fear to rise within. Ask God to make you into a joyful giver, willing to give when the moment is right. God needs people of all economic standings. For now keep a simple list of your possessions and resources. What has God given to you? What could you give away or share with others (maybe not everyone)?

_____

_____

_____

Identity: Scripture reveals the rich and multifaceted identity God has given to you: "child of God," "disciple," "servant," "steward," "temple of the Holy Spirit," and many more. You are called to "be" each of them, embodying both their profound depth and unique specificity for you. For example, you are called to be a "servant," approaching God and people with subservience. You are called to be a "steward," wisely spending your time, money and other gifts from God. As we move ahead, we will investigate further these rich and powerful designations. Begin describing your identity.

_____

_____

_____

Spiritual Gifts are amazing endowments given by the Holy Spirit that are already functioning in your life. Oh yes, you have them. Quite naturally, they supernaturally inspire, motivate and create competence. They empower and equip so that you can effectively serve the Lord and others in everyday life. More than the other attributes, spiritual gifts shape your "call" profile and accompanying attributes. They are like the bone structure of a face. It not only forms a face, but also supports and shapes all the other facial features. Because spiritual gifts are so important, the next chapter is devoted to these extraordinary gifts. You might be surprised and pleased to know that your spiritual gifts are already reflected in what you just recorded. Return here after completing the next chapter and jot down your spiritual gifts.

_____

_____

_____

"So God created humankind in his image, in the image of God he created them; male and female he created them." Genesis 1:27 NRSV

Third Challenge: Summarize Your Unique Attributes

What are your greatest strengths? What stands out as most significant? What surprised you? How do your various attributes connect and intersect with one another? Summarize your findings.

_____

_____

_____

Continue to inventory any new insights and thoughts. Schedule a time on your calendar to revisit this chapter, collecting and recording any new thoughts.

"For we are His workmanship, created in Christ Jesus for good works, which God prepared beforehand so that we would walk in them." Ephesians 2:10 NASB

Prayer: Pray these words from Scripture.

"You have searched me, LORD, and you know me. You know when I sit and when I rise; you perceive my thoughts from afar. You discern my going out and my lying down; you are familiar with all my ways. Before a word is on my tongue you, Lord, know it completely. You hem me in behind and before, and you lay your hand upon me. Such knowledge is too wonderful for me, too lofty for me to attain.

Where can I go from your Spirit? Where can I flee from your presence? If I go up to the heavens, you are there; if I make my bed in the depths, you are there. If I rise on the wings of the dawn, if I settle on the far side of the sea, even there your hand will guide me, your right hand will hold me fast. If I say, 'Surely the darkness will hide me and the light become night around me,' even the darkness will not be dark to you; the night will shine like the day, for darkness is as light to you.

For you created my inmost being; you knit me together in my mother's womb. I praise you because I am fearfully and wonderfully made; your works are wonderful, I know that full well. My frame was not hidden from you when I was made in the secret place, when I was woven together in the depths of the earth. Your eyes saw my unformed body; all the days ordained for me were written in your book before one of them came to be.

How precious to me are your thoughts, God! How vast is the sum of them! Were I to count them, they would outnumber the grains of sand—when I awake, I am still with you." Psalm 139:1-18

Further Thoughts and Actions

- **Study the companion volume, *Custom Designed: A Life Worthy of the Call*.** For real life illustrations and to develop added insight, examine the corresponding chapter.

- **Seek the counsel of a close companion:** If you are so blessed, work through these questions with someone that you trust and who knows you well. You may be surprised by what you learn.

- **Random Thoughts:** Record any new thoughts, feelings, ideas or actions that come to you.

CHAPTER 3
CALLED TO BE GIFTED AND EMPOWERED

....

The Lord is Calling: 1 Corinthians 12; Romans 12:4-8; Ephesians 3:20-4:1, 7, 11-13; Acts 2; Ephesians 5:18; 1 Peter 4:9-10; 1 Timothy 4:14; 2 Timothy 1:6-7; 1 Samuel 16:1-13

Not only does Jesus desire for you to have an extraordinary kingdom influence and impact on the world, but He made it possible by pouring out His Holy Spirit. The Holy Spirit is promised and given to those whom the Lord calls. This was true not only for the Old Testament people, Jesus and the early Christians, but it is true for you:

> *"Repent and be baptized, every one of you, in the name of Jesus Christ for the forgiveness of your sins. And you will receive the gift of the Holy Spirit. The promise is for you and your children and for all who are far off—for all whom the Lord our God will call." Acts 2:38-39*

Not only the early Christians, but people throughout time have witnessed the powerful effect of the Holy Spirit. The Holy Spirit awakens and enlivens the spiritually dead. The Holy Spirit draws people to the living God, causing them to continually repent, receive healing, recognize the Lord's action, desire His forgiveness, speak with power, trust Jesus, and surrender control. Like Jesus, people enlivened and filled with the Holy Spirit still manifest miracles and produce incredible kingdom fruitfulness. Yes, Jesus is still alive, present and working in His body, ordinary people filled with His Spirit, including you. Throughout the Scriptures and even now, the effect of the Holy Spirit is like wine, wind, and fire. Wine, wind and fire when fully set loose are able to have a powerful effect and outcome. Discovering and identifying how the Holy Spirit has empowered you will lead to the same. Maybe you are baptized, yet you're like some early believers who were cautioned:

> "Now concerning spiritual gifts… I do not want you
> to be unaware." 1 Corinthians 12:1 NASB

Still today many are unaware of the Spirit's power and gifts. Bill Hybels, pastor of a very large church, spoke of how he grew up in great churches with great pastors and never heard about spiritual gifts.[1] So, how about you? Do you know how the Holy Spirit has empowered you?

Spiritual gifts are not only pertinent to what you do "at church," but they are meant to empower what you do in your family, work, neighborhood, community, and world. These gifts will intensely motivate and drive you in specific ways. They will cause you to be more focused and effective. When used for Jesus' kingdom purposes, a greater sense of purpose and meaning will result. Often when people first learn about spiritual gifts, they are drawn to the Holy Spirit's power present in these gifts. Many people begin a profound and fun quest to better understand how these gifts function in their lives. Quite miraculously, some people start with little knowledge and later produce unimaginable kingdom fruitfulness. Using these gifts with an understanding of their existence and origin is very exciting and energizing.

Like many terms, "spiritual gift" has various usages. Understanding the distinctions between three definitions will assist you in knowing how the Holy Spirit functions within you. In this chapter, we will focus primarily on the first definition:

1. Spiritual gifts are specific endowments and attributes given by the Holy Spirit that are named and described in Scripture. These gifts quite naturally though really supernaturally motivate and create competence to serve the Lord and others in everyday life.
2. When someone is filled and controlled by the Holy Spirit, then all of one's attributes—talents, skills, words and actions—will operate like a spiritual gift. This is very true also!
3. Everything good in life is a gift from God and is therefore a spiritual gift. This also is very true!

Still today, Jesus is calling and empowering ordinary people for His transformative work in the world. So, how is the Spirit's power at work in you? What are your spiritual gifts? People who are full of the Spirit believe, expect and pray for the miraculous transformative direction and power of the living God Who created the world, raised Jesus from the dead, and is still healing, saving, and transforming a broken world through ordinary people called by Jesus. So, let's press on!

"There are different kinds of gifts, but the same Spirit distributes them. There are different kinds of service, but the same Lord. There are different kinds of working, but in all of them and in everyone it is the same God at work. Now to each one the manifestation of the Spirit is given for the common good." 1 Corinthians 12:4-7

First Challenge: Invite and Welcome the Holy Spirit

The Holy Spirit is already active in your life. Always, the Holy Spirit can be more active. Like the early Christians who already had the Holy Spirit, you also are encouraged:

"Do not get drunk with wine, for that is excessiveness; but be continually filled with the Spirit." Ephesians 5:18 (Author's translation)

Instead of being overly full of wine, you are encouraged to be continually filled, and even overly full of the Holy Spirit. Right now, welcome and invite the Holy Spirit to continually fill you, empowering all of your gifts and attributes. Use the prayer at the end of this chapter. In addition, ask someone to lay hands on you, praying that all your gifts and attributes would be continually filled and empowered by the Holy Spirit. Regularly invite the Holy Spirit to fill and empower you. You cannot accomplish much of eternal significance without the fullness of the Holy Spirit at work within you.

Second Challenge: Identify Your Spiritual Gifts

Complete the Spiritual Gifts Inventory found in Appendix B. The answer sheet is found at the end of this guide, and should be copied or removed. Remember … yes, you already have spiritual gifts! Be honest as you assess yourself. Do not worry about whether your scores are high or low. If you're being forthright, you should expect some or even many low scores.

After completing the inventory, record the three to five spiritual gifts with the highest totals from each of the three sections: "functional" gifts, "manifestional" gifts, and gifts of expression.

_____
_____
_____

"But to each one of us grace has been given as Christ apportioned it. This is why it says: 'When he ascended on high, he took many captives and gave gifts to his people.'" Ephesians 4:7-8

Third Challenge: Investigate Your Spiritual Gifts

Turn to Appendix C and learn about the spiritual gifts that resulted from your inventory. Do the descriptions fit you? Why or why not?

_____
_____
_____

Study the other spiritual gifts described in Appendix C as well. Are any of the other gifts a better fit for you? Why? To which of the other gifts are you drawn or attracted? The inventory is merely an indicator, launching a process of identification. For various reasons, the inventory might not reveal your true gifts.

_____
_____
_____

"For this reason I remind you to continually fan into flame the gift of God, which is in you through the laying on of my hands." 2 Timothy 1:6

Fourth Challenge: Clarify Your Spiritual Gifts

Begin reflecting on how your gifts interrelate. For instance, if you have the spiritual gifts of leadership and mercy, perhaps your leadership gift will be used in a way that also uses your mercy gift, e.g., leading an effort to alleviate hunger. How do your spiritual gifts already shape and relate to one another? In the future, how could your gifts shape and relate to one another?

_____

_____

_____

Now return to your responses captured in Chapter 2. In your responses, is there evidence of your spiritual gifts? Which of your talents, skills and abilities complement and enhance your spiritual gifts? Record your thoughts.

_____

_____

_____

As you reflect upon your life experience (see Chapter 2, Challenge One), what evidence is there of your spiritual gifts? When have you used these gifts? Especially reflect upon life experiences that you enjoyed or were intensely motivated?

_____

_____

_____

Summarize how you have already used your spiritual gifts.

_____

_____

_____

Clarifying your spiritual gifts will meaningfully focus your time. You will know when to say "Yes" and even "No" to various opportunities. For example, maybe you do not have the gifts of leadership or administration, and you're asked to lead a scout group. Immediately you feel overwhelmed by the request. Instead, you would rather serve refreshments or chaperone a camping trip, using your gifts of hospitality, encouragement and shepherding. Feel peace and know that "No" to an opportunity allows another—who will both thrive and be more effective—to say "Yes."

"Each of you should use whatever gift you have received to serve others, as faithful stewards of God's grace in its various forms." 1 Peter 4:10

Fifth Challenge: Continue to Clarify

If you are struggling to clearly identify or better understand your spiritual gifts, choose one or more of the suggestions found on Diagram B. Which of these suggestions will you try?

_____

_____

_____

"Just as each of us has one body with many members, and these members do not all have the same function, so in Christ we, though many, form one body, and each member belongs to all the others. We have different gifts, according to the grace given to each of us." Romans 12:4-6a

God is

R   **Reflect and Recall**: Consider the other unique attributes of your profile and how each complements your spiritual gifts and shapes your call.

E   **Experiment and Examine**: Choose experiences that use your spiritual gifts. If you are using your spiritual gifts, you will feel excited, energized and fulfilled.

V   **Visualize and Imagine**: To which gifts are you drawn, attracted or do you feel an inner pull? As you visualize yourself using your gifts, can you imagine yourself functioning in this way?

E   **Evaluate and Reconsider**: If thinking about spiritual gifts and call is new to you, attend a workshop or talk to someone one-on-one who has an understanding of spiritual gifts.

A   **Affirmation and Input**: What do other people suggest for you, see in you or affirm in you?

L   **Listen and Pray**: Ask God, "What are you calling me to do?" Ask God for wisdom and personal vision and revelation.

I   **Inventory and Assess**: Try one or more spiritual gifts inventories.

N   **Nurture and Grow**: Most important, seek to know follow and serve Jesus.

G   **Gather and Learn**: Learn as much as you can about spiritual gifts.

Your SPIRITUAL GIFTS to You!

Diagram B

Sixth Challenge: Adjust Your Attitude

It's important to realize spiritual gifts are given for "loving" and "serving" the Lord and others—not for selfish, arrogant or egotistical ends. In the middle of a long discussion on spiritual gifts, the apostle Paul warned that having supernatural gifts without love is meaningless (1 Corinthians 13). With love, Jesus both could challenge someone to something better, and uplift yet another needing comfort and encouragement.

Though Jesus was the living God, teacher, leader, and prophet, he demonstrated servanthood, taking a basin and towel, and washing the disciples' feet. It was a humbling, menial and dirty task. Much of the time, you will serve using your spiritual gifts. Still though, there will be times when something is "needed," and seemingly no one wants to do it (Be careful how you define "needed"). At these times, the Lord is calling you to take a "towel and basin" as a servant, and complete what is needed. Define servant. How will you live as a loving servant?

_____

_____

_____

Constantly remembering you are Jesus' servant hopefully will result in a humble attitude and accurate assessment of yourself. Jesus told his disciples including you:

"You call me 'Teacher' and 'Lord,' and rightly so, for that is what I am. Now that I, your Lord and Teacher, have washed your feet, you also should wash one another's feet. I have set you an example that you should do as I have done for you. Very truly I tell you, no servant is greater than his master, nor is a messenger greater than the one who sent him." John 13:13-16

Seventh Challenge: Try an "Elevator Speech"

If you have in earnest invested time and effort, challenging yourself, you should better understand your unique "call" profile and how the Holy Spirit has already equipped and empowered you. Your unique profile will answer the question: "Who am I?" It's a serious start, providing significant insight as you seek the Lord's call.

In my business profession, a meaningful exercise for me was to develop an "elevator speech." The idea is not mine, but I have found it to be helpful in building a confident understanding of my work's fundamental purpose.

The "elevator speech" works like this: If I was traveling between two floors on an elevator and was asked, *"What do you do for a living?"* I could share more than a simple response such as *"salesman," "plumber,"* or *"lawyer."* I would be prepared to say, *"I am a district representative for a major technology company that specializes in network technology,"* or *"I am a problem solver in the form of a business attorney that specializes in resolving difficult disputes."*

Now take an imaginary elevator ride. In a sentence or two or short paragraph, write an elevator speech, answering the question: "Who am I?" With your response, summarize your unique "call" profile developed in Chapters 2 and 3.

_____

_____

_____

Be confident! Even though you may need some time to clarify your spiritual gifts, God has already supernaturally equipped and empowered you.

"Do not neglect your gift which was given to you…" 1 Timothy 4:14

Prayer: Continually invite the Holy Spirit to enliven and empower you. Pray this prayer from the Scripture and tradition, expecting the Lord to act.

"Gracious Lord, through water and the Spirit you have made me your own. You forgave me all my sins and brought me to newness of life. Continue to strengthen me with the Holy Spirit: the spirit of wisdom and understanding, the spirit of counsel and might, the spirit of knowledge and fear of the Lord, the spirit of joy in your presence. Daily increase in me your gifts of grace. For Jesus sake, fan into flame the gift of your Holy Spirit; confirm my faith, guide my life, empower me in my serving, give me patience in suffering and bring me to everlasting life. AMEN"[2]

Further Thoughts and Actions

- Study the companion volume, *Custom Designed: A Life Worthy of the Call*. For real life illustrations and to develop added insight, examine the corresponding chapter.

- Study the spiritual gift lists found in Scripture:

    Romans 12:1-8
    1 Corinthians 12
    Ephesians 4:1-16
    1 Peter 4:10

- **Learn more about spiritual gifts by reading a book.** Here is a suggestion:

  Your Spiritual Gifts Can Help Your Church Grow
  by C. Peter Wagner

- **Random Thoughts:** Record any thoughts, feelings, ideas or actions that come to you.

THE PLACES

YOUR UNIQUE MISSION FIELD!

Jesus is concerned about all places. Not only has Jesus given you His power to prepare you, but Jesus also has prepared the places where He will call and send you. Jesus called and sent out the twelve disciples, giving them authority and power to speak and do as He did (Luke 9). Later He "sent" out still more of his followers:

"After this the Lord appointed seventy-two others and sent them two by two ahead of him to every town and place where he was about to go. He told them, ' The harvest is plentiful, but the workers are few. Ask the Lord of the harvest, therefore, to send out workers into his harvest field. Go! I am sending you out like lambs among wolves.'" Luke 10:1-3

There will never be enough "workers" for the harvest "field." That's why the Lord needs you to: *"Go!"* So where is Jesus "sending" you and what is He calling you to do? What is your harvest "field?"

In Latin, the word for "send" is *misseo* from which we get the word, "mission." Jesus was a "missionary," "sent" by the Father. The Father sent Jesus to accomplish his will and ways in His harvest field—that is His "mission" field. In turn, Jesus enlisted many others. As He was preparing to leave His life on earth, he said to them:

"Peace be with you! As the Father has sent me, I am sending you." John 20:21

Now it's your turn! Though you may not go to a foreign land, you also have a mission field ripe for harvest. Every day, the Lord calls and "sends" you "out" into the unique "mission" field of your life: home, work (school), community, world, and the gathering of believers that you label "church." Remember though, really church is you and every other ordinary person who trusts in Jesus. You are the church, the "called out ones" … 24/7. You're "called out" by Jesus into all the places of your mission field to speak and do as He did. How will you live worthy of Jesus and His call in the mission field of your unique life: your home, work, neighborhood, community, world and your church gathering?

The Places

Incorporate the Lord's call into the unique mission field of your life!

Chapter 4   Call to Work, Family, Church, Neighborhood, Community and World

CHAPTER 4
CALL TO WORK, FAMILY, CHURCH, NEIGHBORHOOD, COMMUNITY AND WORLD

The Lord is Calling: Luke 9:1-2; Luke 10:1-12, 25-37; Acts 1:8; John 20:21; 1 Peter 1:15-16; 1 Peter 2:4-9; Psalm 37:4-5

Jesus gives us His power and everything needed to live worthy of His call in the places where He "sends" us. So, do you know the places where the Lord is sending you—your unique mission field? Do you know what He is calling you to "be" and "do" in these places?

"But just as he who called you is holy, so be holy in all you do; for it is written: ' Be holy, because I am holy.'" 1 Peter 1:15-16

Jesus is calling you to *"be holy in all you do."* Holiness is being dedicated to the Lord and His purposes in the roles and places of life where He is sending you. These places are shown at the bottom of Diagram A (in Chapter 1). The Lord desires that we would dedicate all these places to His purposes. The Lord calls you to use His power and gifts in all these places: your work, family, the church gathering, neighborhood, community and world.

Jesus is concerned about all the places of your life. Have you dedicated these places to His kingdom purposes? Maybe your unique mission field is ripe for the harvest. So let's press on!

"He has saved us and called us to a holy life—not because of anything we have done but because of his own purpose and grace. This grace was given us in Christ Jesus before the beginning of time, but it has now been revealed through the appearing of our Savior, Christ Jesus, who has destroyed death and has brought life and immortality to light through the gospel." 2 Timothy 1:9-10

First Challenge: Identify Your Mission Field

Identify the places where God has already sent you: your mission field.

List your family roles. Here are a few examples: father, sister, son, aunt, cousin or wife.

_____

_____

List your roles at work: engineer, doctor, supervisor, student, friend, or co-worker.

_____

_____

List your roles in your neighborhood, community and world: neighbor, school board, Girl Scout leader, hospital volunteer, missionary, city council, chamber of commerce, or politician.

_____

_____

List your roles in your church gathering: council leader, adult teacher, hospitality greeter, usher, choir member, event coordinator, or children's worker.

_____

_____

Jesus expressed this desire for you:

"I came that they may have life, and have it abundantly." John 10:10b

Second Challenge: Seek the Lord's Desires

In Scripture, we find a helpful promise as we seek the Lord's call:

"Take delight in the Lord, and he will give you the desires of your heart. Commit your way to the Lord; trust in him and he will do this." Psalm 37:4-5

As you take delight in the Lord, He will plant His desires in your heart. When Jesus truly inspires these desires, they also will clarify His call. Identifying them will paint a powerful kingdom vision for the places of your unique mission field, shaping your goals and priorities. In addition, these desires likely will not change over time.

Commit your way to the Lord, dedicating it to His purposes. Invite Him to plant His desires in your heart. Then begin to identify and record these desires. Writing will bring greater clarity. Get started! This exercise may take some time to complete, maybe even weeks or months. Make a date on your calendar to return in a week or even a month. What are the desires that the Lord has planted in your heart for the following?

Your Relationship with Jesus

_____

_____

_____

Work (or School): What are the desires of your heart for your work, both now and in the future? What is your vocation presently? Where do you use your spiritual gifts, if at all? What tasks and activities do you most enjoy? What do you least enjoy? Chances are good that less enjoyable activities do not use your spiritual gifts. Perhaps you can shift these responsibilities to someone else. How would you answer these questions for jobs you have held in the past even when you were very young, or employed in seemingly useless jobs? What are the desires of your heart?

_____

_____

_____

Family and Home: What are the desires of your heart for marriage? What do you desire for your children? What do you desire for your home and the management of it? What do you desire for your friendships? How could you improve these relationships? How do you use your spiritual gifts in your home? If you are not married, list desirable characteristics and attributes for a spouse. Which desires are non-negotiable?

_____

_____

_____

Neighborhood, Community and World: Your "neighbor" is anyone that your life affects (Luke 10:25-37; Acts 1:8). What are your desires for neighborhood, community and world? Where could you have a transformative influence, meaningfully using your spiritual gifts and talents in your neighborhood? How about in your community, city or region? How about in the world?

_____

_____

_____

Church Gathering, the "Called Out Ones:" What do you desire for your church gathering? What would you like your roles or function to be? How could you encourage and enable ordinary people to be mobilized and "called out" to transform the world? How could you effectively employ your spiritual gifts? How could you multiply what is already happening or even launch something new? What would you like to stop doing in order to invest your time differently?

_____

_____

_____

Your Personal Growth

_____

_____

_____

Your Character

_____

_____

_____

Your Emotional Well Being

_____

_____

_____

Your Physical Well Being

_____
_____
_____

Your Finances and Material Goods

_____
_____
_____

Your Leisure Time: Hobbies and Fun

_____
_____
_____

Your Retirement

_____
_____
_____

Be encouraged! Even though you may be exhausted, know that you have done valuable work. Your responses will be helpful tools for living worthy of Jesus and His call. Mark your calendar to return later.

"Take delight in the Lord, and he will give you the desires of your heart. Commit your way to the Lord; trust in him and he will do this:" Psalm 37:4-5

Third Challenge: Another "Elevator Speech"

Now take another imaginary elevator ride. So far, how would you respond to this question: *"What is the Lord calling you to be and do?"* Summarize your response with another "elevator speech" (See Chapter 3, Challenge 7 for more explanation).

_____

_____

_____

_____

_____

The Lord will continue to inspire your thoughts and inner promptings, giving you further revelation. As you seek and search, prayerfully reflect on these powerful words:

> *"'The Lord is my shepherd, I shall not want. He makes me lie down in green pastures; he leads me beside still waters; he restores my soul. He leads me in right paths for his name's sake." Psalm 23:1-3 NRSV*

Prayer: Picture Jesus with you. Then offer each desire of your heart to the Lord, talking to Him about each one.

Further Thoughts and Actions

- Study the companion volume, *Custom Designed: A Life Worthy of the Call.* For real life illustrations and to develop added insight, examine the corresponding chapter.

- **Sample Ideas:** Let your mind wander and sample new ideas for each place of your unique mission field. Try on these ideas. Do they fit you? Does this small sampling energize you? Consider why or why not. What is uncomfortable? Try a small task or short-term assignment to confirm whether these new ideas fit you.

- **Create a Personal Mission Statement(s):** Similar to a corporation or church, write a personal mission statement. A mission statement can focus your life. Write several mission statements for your work, family, church, neighborhood, community and world.

- **Random Thoughts:** Record any thoughts, feelings, ideas or actions that come to you.

THE PLAN

GOD AND ORDINARY PEOPLE LIKE YOU!

You are an important person in God's plan. Throughout time, the Lord has personally partnered with human flesh to heal and transform a broken world … this is His plan! Jesus the Word made flesh, most clearly revealed His Father's purposeful plan. Not long after Jesus was baptized and "anointed" with the Holy Spirit's power, he began calling and training others to participate in His Father's plan:

> "From that time on Jesus began to preach, 'Repent, for the kingdom of heaven has come near.' As Jesus was walking beside the Sea of Galilee, he saw two brothers, Simon called Peter and his brother Andrew. They were casting a net into the lake, for they were fishermen. 'Come, follow me,' Jesus said, 'and I will send you out to fish for people.' At once they left their nets and followed him. Going on from there, he saw two other brothers, James son of Zebedee and his brother John. They were in a boat with their father Zebedee, preparing their nets. Jesus called them, and immediately they left the boat and their father and followed him." Matthew 4:17-22

As Jesus spoke and demonstrated His Father's purposes, He gathered a group of ordinary people, forming relationships and partnering with them, calling and training them to accomplish His Father's intentions. They were not just servants and followers of Jesus, but also His friends. Through knowing and following Him, Jesus taught and trained these apprentices. They were His disciples. Disciple means learner or apprentice. Jesus is calling you to be His disciple. Jesus longs to be your friend so that He can teach and train you.

Still today, Jesus is alive and calling ordinary people like you to know, follow and serve Him. Personal and deep relationships are still His priority! Jesus is still enlisting and partnering with people to participate in His Father's plan. He is still befriending, training, empowering and sending out His disciples to transform people, problems and places. This is His plan!

The Plan

Jesus is calling you! Know follow and serve Him! Be His apprentice! Hear Him speak! With others, participate in His plan!

Chapter 5   Called to the Greatest Relationship
Chapter 6   Called to Inspiration
Chapter 7   Called to Support and Trust

CHAPTER 5
CALLED TO THE GREATEST RELATIONSHIP

The Lord is Calling: Matthew 4:17-22; Matthew 28:18-20; Luke 9:57-62; John 15; John 17:3; Romans 8:30; 1 Corinthians 1:9; Philippians 3:7-14

First things first. You are called to the greatest relationship possible … better than the best friendship or the perfect marriage. Relationship with Jesus is essential and indispensable. Jesus is calling, befriending and partnering with ordinary people … this is God's plan!

> *"God is faithful, who has called you into fellowship with his Son,*
> *Jesus Christ our Lord." 1 Corinthians 1:9*

The Biblical Greek word for "fellowship" is *koininia*. *Koininia* describes deep relationships where people know each other well. *Koininia* relationships are characterized by significant trust where people mutually share their lives with one another including their time, thoughts, feelings, burdens, insecurities, joys, brokenness, and sometimes even possessions. In human relationships, we get a taste of *koininia;* however, the most complete and greatest *koininia* relationship possible is with Jesus, and Jesus is calling you to a *koininia* relationship.

A *koininia* relationship with Jesus is unlike all other relationships. You receive unending forgiveness and unconditional love. You are transformed and trained to live worthy of Jesus and in conformity with His call. You receive wisdom and guidance, experience joy, find the meaning of life, receive healing, and are the kind of person that most people would want to be.

When you are in relationship with Jesus, you are a beloved child of the Heavenly Father and part of a royal family. In this family, you have inherited all the riches of His blessings. These blessings include not only material resources, but also salvation, forgiveness of sins, God's word, many family and friends, hope and much more. In fact, everything good is a gift from the Father who longs to give and give and never stop giving to His family. All this undeserved giving is called grace and it's for you.

When I once investigated every "call" scripture, I discovered the Lord's call could be summarized by a few words found on the top of Diagram A in Chapter 1: You are called to *know, follow* and *serve* Jesus. In fact knowing, following and serving Jesus in a *koininia* relationship is all that is needed for life. It's putting first things first.

"I keep asking that the God of our Lord Jesus Christ, the glorious Father, may give you the Spirit of wisdom and revelation, so that you may know him better. I pray that the eyes of your heart may be enlightened in order that you may know the hope to which he has called you, the riches of his glorious inheritance in his holy people, and his incomparably great power for us who believe." Ephesians 1:17-19a

First Challenge: Relationship with Jesus?

"Know" is a curious word. You may "know" a fair amount *about* someone and still not "know" them as a friend. This may be true of Jesus as well. You might "know" a lot *about* Jesus, but not really "know" Him, at least not very well. Do you know Jesus? Invite Jesus to be your best friend. Trust Him now if you have not already. Describe the current state of your relationship with Jesus. Does the word *koininia* describe your relationship? Why or why not? What do you desire for your relationship with Jesus?

_____

_____

_____

Jesus has made an incredible promise to you:

"And surely I am with you always, to the very end of the age." Matthew 28:20b

Second Challenge: Recall Your Love at First

It is also possible that you knew Jesus at one time but over time your relationship has deteriorated. Currently you may feel distant from Him. The Lord spoke to some early believers who were in a similar state:

"Yet I hold this against you: You have forsaken the love you had at first. Consider how far you have fallen! Repent and do the things you did at first. If you do not repent, I will come to you and remove your lampstand from its place." Revelation 2:4-5

Perhaps this prophetic word is a needed word for you. When were you first conscious of your love for Jesus? Describe your love for Him then. When was the highpoint of your love for Jesus? Describe your love then. Is there a contrast as you consider your present relationship with Jesus? Why or why not?

_____

_____

_____

No matter what, the Heavenly Father promises to love you:

"See what great love the Father has lavished on us, that we should be called children of God! And that is what we are!" 1 John 3:1a

Third Challenge: Jesus Longs to Forgive You

When people are "in love," they will go out of their way and use extraordinary means to put their lover first. Jesus also knew some secrets about love. He once experienced the love of a weeping woman while at Simon the Pharisee's house:

"As she stood behind Jesus at his feet weeping, she began to wet his feet with her tears and she wiped them with her hair, kissed them and poured perfume on them."

Simon the Pharisee was not impressed, labeling this woman a "sinner." Jesus responded by telling Simon a parable:

"Two people owed money to a certain moneylender. One owed him five hundred denarii, and the other fifty. Neither of them had the money to pay him back, so he forgave the debts of both. 'Now which of them will love him more?'
Simon replied, 'I suppose the one who had the bigger debt forgiven.'
'You have judged correctly,' Jesus said." Luke 7:41-43

This weeping woman knew she owed a big debt to the Lord, and yet she owed absolutely nothing because she had been forgiven. She could not help but express her love and gratefulness.

So how much do you owe God? Let's consider this question. Think about the last few days. Sit in silence. When have you spoken harmful and hurtful words? When have your actions caused pain and evil? How about your thoughts and relationships? When have you abandoned or forgotten Jesus and His ways? Take your time with these questions. Ask the Holy Spirit to reveal the answers. Take inventory by specifically writing your responses. Then find a hammer, nails and a block of wood. Drive a nail into the wood for each item you have written. Now contemplate all the sins committed on the multitude of other days throughout your life. Your sins caused the nails to be driven, crucifying Jesus on a cruel cross. How does this make you feel? Share your reflections.

_____

_____

_____

You may not like the word sin. In fact I really do not like it either. It puts me in touch with all that I really do not like about myself. Unless you know that your sins caused the death of Jesus, you will never realize how much you need Him. If you are really serious in your self-examination, you will know that you are deeply indebted to Him. You owe the Lord much for how you have gone astray, abandoning Him and His ways; however, this is not all of what you owe Him. You also owe Him for every good thing in your life. Amazingly however, though you owe the Lord for everything, you owe Him absolutely nothing. Why? It's because your massive debt has been forgiven at great cost to the Lord, but absolutely free to you. How does this make you feel?

_____

_____

_____

The longer I know Jesus, the more I realize how desperately I need Him and how I could never get along without Him. At times I trick myself, thinking that I do pretty well at measuring up to His standards; however if

I am truly honest, I am only fooling myself. My sins create a considerable dividing wall between the living God and me. We all know the reality of a dividing wall and how it feels. God's Son Jesus has destroyed the dividing wall, dying on a cruel cross for you and me. With great mercy and costly love, Jesus cried out to you:

"Father forgive them; for they do not know what they are doing." Luke 23:34

Fourth Challenge: Know Jesus More

Similar to any friendship, you can know Jesus, and still you can always know Him better … more deeply and personally.

Many years ago when I felt challenged by some questions, I sought out a pastor friend. This pastor friend said: *"I can tell that you are someone who wants to love and serve God; so, don't worry so much about your questions. Don't even think about them. Instead, make it your No. 1 goal in life to know Jesus and then all else will fall into place."* Perhaps this advice was simplistic; yet, it's the best advice I have ever received. Whether life is good or not so good, the Lord over and over reminds me of this advice: *"Make it your No. 1 goal in life to know Jesus and then all else will fall into place."* I hope that knowing Jesus is so valuable to you that it will be your No. 1 priority and goal in life.

"Knowing Jesus" … is this your No. 1 goal in life? Why or why not? How is this reflected in how you "spend" your life, your priorities and time?

_____

_____

_____

Jesus is calling you to the greatest relationship imaginable. Unlike all other relationships, Jesus is completely trustworthy. Similar to marriage, the living Lord has entered into an everlasting covenant with you. Unlike all marriages, the Lord is a perfect covenant keeper. Unlike all politicians, only the Lord can deliver on all of His promises.

Spend five minutes with Jesus. Picture Him with you. Rest in His love and imagine it embracing you. Slowly read and prayerfully reflect upon this promise from Scripture:

"His divine power has given us everything we need for life and godliness through our knowledge of him who called us by his own glory and goodness. Through these he has given us his very great and precious promises, so that through them you may participate in the divine nature and escape the corruption in the world caused by evil desires. For this very reason, make every effort to add to your faith goodness; and to goodness, knowledge." 2 Peter 1:3-5

What is Jesus saying to you?

_____

_____

_____

We come to know and experience the living Jesus through spending time with Him. Daily, how could you spend at least five minutes with Jesus? Make a commitment. Finding the time and making it happen is perhaps the biggest challenge. Spending time with Jesus who can do great things in your life or doing something far less significant like watching TV, which do you believe will yield the better result? When could you do this … in the morning, evening or maybe the first available time in your day when other things can wait till later? What needs to change to make it happen?

_____

_____

_____

What will you do to get to know Jesus better? Which of these practices might be helpful? How will you make it happen? Be specific.

- Hearing Jesus speak through His living active word: Scripture
- Being in Jesus' presence
- Bowing down and worshipping Jesus—regularly
- Praying: Having a continual conversation with Jesus, talking and listening
- Being with Jesus and His friends at His table: Eating "bread and wine" to remember Him and His unconditional love
- Being together with other people who also know Jesus

_____

_____

_____

Reflect upon these life-giving words of Jesus:

"Now this is eternal life: that they know you, the only true God, and Jesus Christ, whom you have sent." John 17:3

Fifth Challenge: Build Trust

The Biblical Greek word for faith can be translated *"trust,"* implying relationship. Jesus' first followers must have perceived something compelling in Jesus, causing them to trust Him. Because when He "called" them, they left all and *"immediately followed."* (Matthew 4:17)

"Follow" can be a scary word because of what it implies. How does the word "follow" make you feel?

_____

_____

_____

Often fear is the greatest hurdle to following Jesus. Some of my close friends once expressed a fear. They feared that God might want them to go to *"Oogaboogaland,"* and they freely admitted that they didn't want to go to *"Oogaboogaland."*

"Oogaboogaland" represents the one thing that Jesus might ask of you that you would never want to do and of course if you did it, the most miserable outcome would occur. This is such a common fear I am convinced that Satan, the author of fear has no creativity. So what does *"Oogaboogaland"* represent for you? What do you fear most about following Jesus? How does this fear affect you? Be honest! Exposing fear dispels its power.

_____

_____

_____

We fear the unknown or that Jesus will deal us a royal bummer or that we will turn into the kind of person that we would never want to be. Forget it! Jesus did not give you a *"spirit of fear"* (2 Timothy 1:7). Jesus tells you over and over: *"Do not be afraid."*

For anyone to truly want to follow Jesus, the truth needs to be clear. A deeper trust is needed. Jesus is not like any human person you may know. Jesus is not a hard taskmaster or harsh criticizer. Jesus is not a robber, longing to take from you. Neither is Jesus a vending machine, producing upon demand all the things that you are sure you need right now. To be fully assured of these truths, Jesus told us over and over who He was. Which of these promises spoken by Jesus capture you?

"I am the bread of life. Whoever comes to me will never go hungry, and whoever believes in me will never be thirsty." John 6:35

"I am the light of the world. Whoever follows me will never walk in darkness, but will have the light of life." John 8:12

"The thief comes only to steal and kill and destroy; I have come that they may have life, and have it to the full. I am the good shepherd. The good shepherd lays down his life for the sheep. ...I know my sheep and my sheep know me." John 10:10-11, 14b

"I am the resurrection and the life. Those who believe in me, even though they die, will live, and everyone who lives and believes in me will never die." John 11:25-26 NRSV

"I am the way and the truth and the life. No one comes to the Father except through me." John 14:6 NRSV

"I am the vine; you are the branches. Those who abide in me and I in them bear much fruit, because apart from me you can do nothing." John 15:5

Which of these *"I am"* promises of Jesus captures your attention? Spend another five minutes with Jesus, picturing Him with you and His love surrounding you. Slowly read and prayerfully reflect one word at a time upon one of these *"I am"* promises. What thoughts is Jesus putting in your mind? What is He saying to you?

_____

_____

_____

Often God's people have recounted the past, praising and thanking the Lord for what He has given them and accomplished on their behalf (For example: Psalm 107). As God's people recalled His past blessings, their trust in the Lord and hope for the future increased. In like manner, recall or "count" your blessings. Recall all that makes life wonderful, simple or great. Make a list. I once did this and my list had nearly one hundred items on it in a few minutes. To get you started, here are a few examples from my list: a living and loving God, loving family, many loyal friends (I listed each of them), encouragement, several wise mentors, faithful prayer people, Jesus' forgiveness and salvation, sports, freedom, creativity, chocolate, and Italian food, etc. What is your list of blessings?

_____

_____

_____

As you review your list of blessings, what happens within you?

_____

_____

_____

Jesus deeply loves you, and graciously gives you all that you need and more. Jesus was present at the beginning of creation, and He was present at your creation. Jesus is utterly brilliant. He knows every detail about you, and if that is not enough, every other person! Jesus is speaking these words to you:

"Indeed, the very hairs of your head are all numbered. Don't be afraid; you are worth more than many sparrows." Luke 12:7

Sixth Challenge: Follow Jesus

As you more deeply and personally come to know Jesus, hopefully you will want nothing else than to follow Him step by step by step. Sometimes like a foggy road, life is confusing. Jesus longs to lead and guide you through the fog. As His disciple (apprentice), He will teach and train you for life. Jesus told His original apprentices:

"Not everyone who says to me, 'Lord, Lord,' will enter the kingdom of heaven, but only the one who does the will of my Father who is in heaven... Therefore everyone who hears these words of mine and puts them into practice is like a wise man who built his house on the rock. The rain came down, the streams rose, and the winds blew and beat against that house; yet it did not fall, because it had its foundation on the rock. But everyone who hears these words of mine and does not put them into practice is like a foolish man who built his house on sand. The rain came down, the streams rose, and the winds blew and beat against that house, and it fell with a great crash."
Matthew 7:21, 24-27

Jesus desires for us to put His words into "practice." To become a "master" of anything, whether playing the piano or becoming a "master" electrician, "practice," "discipline" and training from a "master" teacher are required. Jesus' apprentices also need "practice" and "discipline." "Practice" and "discipline" require repetition and refinement.

"Lord" literally means "Master." The Master, Jesus, will teach and train you through many practical and time-tested scriptural "disciplines" that He and His other followers have "practiced" throughout the centuries. These disciplines are not for earning His love and salvation; rather through "practicing" them, Jesus gives His grace, transforming your thoughts, words and deeds into His likeness and setting you free. Here is a sampling of these "disciplines and practices:"

- Meditation: Listening for Jesus and reflecting upon His word
- Prayer: Conversation with the living God—talking and listening
- Study of God's word and work in creation in order to know the truth that sets us free
- Fasting: Abstaining from food or some practice for the purpose of inward transformation
- Solitude: Ceasing from crowds, noise and activity in order to commune with the Lord
- Submission: Inner attitude of mutual subordination and not demanding one's own way
- Service: Freely and inwardly giving up one's rights and position through loving action
- Simplicity: Inward focus upon Jesus alone that leads to contentment and an outward lifestyle (Chapter 10)
- Guidance: Listening to feedback from Jesus' followers (Chapter 7)
- Confession: Self-examination followed by honest and specific acknowledgment before the Lord and others (Chapters 11)
- Worship: Inward posture of bowing down to the living God and acknowledging His worth
- Celebration: Joy and freedom resulting from the "practice" of these "disciplines"[3]

Which of these "practices and disciplines" seems most familiar? Which is most puzzling? Which do you already "practice?" Which one or two do you want to "practice" more regularly?

_____

_____

_____

Some of these life-giving "practices" are intentionally introduced in other chapters of this guide. In addition, I highly recommend the well-known book *Celebration of Discipline* by Richard Foster in order to add more depth to your understanding and "practice." Jesus made this promise:

"If you continue in my word, you are truly my disciples; and you will know the truth, and the truth will make you free." John 8:31b-32 NRSV

Seventh Challenge: Know Follow Serve Jesus in All of Life

The words, *know, follow,* and *serve* describe a progression that is not a progression of time. For when you are called to know Jesus, simultaneously you are called to follow and serve Him. I use the scriptural image of a house to describe this progression. Like the foundation of a house, the call to know Jesus is most fundamental. Following Jesus is like building the house's walls. In turn, serving Jesus is what makes the house unique. A house built without a foundation or walls will not withstand the storms of life. However if your serving naturally results from knowing and following Jesus, it quite likely will have eternal significance.

Jesus calls you to know follow and serve Him in all of life. This includes not only what is seen outwardly, but also your inner thoughts, character, attitudes and relationships. Often what is inward precedes what is seen outwardly. So, what is happening with your inner thoughts, character, attitudes and relationships? What does the Lord need to transform? What "practices or disciplines" might help?

_____

_____

_____

"For we are co-workers in God's service; you are God's field, God's building. By the grace God has given me, I laid a foundation as a wise builder, and someone else is building on it. But each one should build with care. For no one can lay any foundation other than the one already laid, which is Jesus Christ." 1 Corinthians 3:9-11

Eighth Challenge: The Lord is Pursuing You!

Talk to someone that you respect about your relationship with Jesus … perhaps a pastor, spiritual director or a good Christian friend. Discuss any of the challenges from this chapter. Ask them for wisdom on how to develop your relationship with Jesus into the greatest of all possible relationships. Jot down notable ideas.

_____

_____

_____

At this point, if something about Jesus' call is bothersome, consider this: Jesus will not stop calling you! In fact, Jesus' call is like a constantly ringing telephone. Jesus is always calling you, constantly beckoning and pursuing you, never forcing you, but continually trying to get your attention, constantly trying to reach out to you, and always offering to you a relationship with Himself. As a result, I am sure that you have already sensed His call. How do these words make you feel? How have you seen the living God at work in your life? What gets in the way?

_____

_____

_____

Jesus is continually and constantly "searching" for you like the woman who is searching in this parable:

"Or what woman having ten silver coins, if she loses one of them, does not light a lamp, sweep the house, and search carefully until she finds it? When she has found it, she calls together her friends and neighbors, saying, 'Rejoice with me, for I have found the coin that I had lost." Luke 15:8-9 NRSV

Prayer: Write a letter to the Lord. Pray and talk to Jesus as you write. In this letter, share your deepest desires for life. Offer to Jesus your hopes and dreams. Ask the Lord to help you where you trip and fall. Ask Him for what you most need. Invite Jesus to be involved and work in every aspect of your life. Thank Him for what He has already done in your life and all the many gifts that you have received. When finished, pray the entire letter. Consider praying it daily or keep a journal where you continually write letters to Him.

Further Thoughts and Actions

- Study the companion volume, *Custom Designed: A Life Worthy of the Call*. For real-life illustrations and to develop added insight, examine the corresponding chapter.

- **Find a church gathering.** If you do not have a church gathering, find one and go regularly: If you try a church gathering and you do not like it, try another. Keep trying until you find one that fits you. Look for a church gathering where you experience and grow in knowing Jesus (as revealed in Scripture) who is for you and not against you. Seek a church gathering where you feel comfortable and you can be yourself. Find a church where you know that your failures and sins are forgiven—past, present and future. Look for a church gathering where you continually hear and learn God's truthful and trustworthy words from Scripture. Find a church gathering where you are helped, encouraged, inspired and even challenged at times. Seek a church gathering that prays and expects Jesus' healing and miraculous power. Remember church is not an institution, but rather a group of imperfect people like you. Because people are imperfect, not all these characteristics will be present all the time. Once you find the right church gathering, commit to staying, gathering and worshipping regularly.

- **Learn more by reading a book.** Here are some favorites:

    1. *My Heart, Christ's Home* by Robert Boyd Munger
       This short booklet describes and invites "knowing" Jesus.
    2. *Sit Walk Stand* by Watchman Nee
       Concise teaching on life with Jesus, based upon Ephesians
    3. *Celebration of Discipline* by Richard Foster
       Teaching on the classical spiritual disciplines

- **Study the life of Jesus in the Gospel writings of the New Testament.**

- **Be Baptized.** If you have never been baptized, entrust your life to the Lord, receive instruction and be baptized.

- **Consider what hinders you.** What hinders you from knowing, following and serving Jesus? Why? Peruse the list below. Talk with a trustworthy companion. If needed, shout at God. Be honest. Be angry. Cry or even weep. God can handle all of our emotions. These feelings and prayers are normal human reactions that are present in the Psalms and other Scripture. Write your own psalm, prayer or letter.

- Maybe you feel forsaken or you feel like you have been dealt a horrible lot in life (Psalms 22 and 46).
- Maybe someone has deeply hurt you (Psalms 35 and 34).
- Maybe you are angry with God about something (Psalm 13:1-4).
- Maybe you know religious people that you really do not like. You do not need to be like them (Philippians 1:15-18).
- Maybe you have regrets (Psalm 51).
- Maybe you feel trapped by something (Psalm 102:8-11).
- Maybe your experience of church has been all about running an organization or getting you to do certain things or getting your money or building a building (2 Timothy 3:5).
- Maybe you do not like or believe part or all of the Bible for one reason or another (2 Corinthians 4:2).
- Maybe you do not like certain religious words (Job 26:1-4).

_____

_____

_____

Picture the Lord with you right now as you reflect upon these words:

"I lift up my eyes to the hills—from where will my help come? My help comes from the LORD, who made heaven and earth." Psalm 121:1-2 NRSV

- **Random Thoughts:** Record any thoughts, feelings, ideas or actions that come to you.

CHAPTER 6
CALLED TO INSPIRATION

The Lord is Calling: 1 Kings 19:11-16; Proverbs 3:5-6; Psalm 32:8-9; John 10:1-18; Mark 4:1-20; Hebrews 4:12-16; 1 Thessalonians 5:17

"Call" and relationship imply communication and conversation. Relationship with Jesus is no exception. Remember prayer is a conversation, both talking and listening. Jesus' call must be heard and the key to hearing is listening. Jesus knew that his followers would know and recognize His voice:

"When he has brought out all his own, he goes on ahead of them, and his sheep follow him because they know his voice. But they will never follow a stranger; in fact, they will run away from him because they do not recognize a stranger's voice." John 10:4-5

Jesus is still alive and speaking. If you would like to hear Jesus' call and partner with Him in His plan, then you will need to recognize His voice and discern His guidance. Can you recognize His voice? The Holy Spirit can personally, practically and specifically speak, guiding you as well.

Many years ago like many young parents, one day I felt overwhelmed and insecure in my new parenting role. While contemplating some of Jesus' words from Scripture (Luke 12:22-32), the Holy Spirit inspired a thought in me: *"If you honestly and specifically acknowledge your wrongs and humbly ask for forgiveness from your children, then your relationship with them will be fine."* I suddenly felt reassured and filled with deep peace. In fact this wisdom has been very helpful and applicable to other relationships as well. In a similar way throughout the years, Jesus has spoken to me, often through Scripture. Through "practice," I have learned to recognize the Lord's voice. Note that "listening" is in the center of Diagram A (in Chapter 1).

In many and various ways throughout time, the living God has spoken—even in an audible voice to a small few. As you seek to know, follow and serve Jesus, He will guide you, speaking and helping you to see ahead. Jesus will speak through Scripture and many time-tested "practices," particularly meditative prayer. The Holy Spirit inside of you will gently whisper to you, inspiring your thoughts and using the still small voice inside of you. Jesus' Spirit might prompt or nudge with a strong conviction, a clear inward impression, a deep motivation or desire, intense thought, excitement about pursuing something, a deep knowing, a feeling of being drawn to something, or a waterfall of new words, thoughts or ideas—filled with wisdom, grace and truth for you. Only Jesus' Spirit can invent truly innovative and creative thoughts. Learn to recognize Jesus' voice, and He will spontaneously inspire you.

"I pray that the eyes of your heart may be enlightened in order that you may know the hope to which he has called you, the riches of his glorious inheritance in his holy people, and his incomparably great power for us who believe." Ephesians 1:18-19a

First Challenge: Quiet the Noise

Have you had the joy of hearing the gentle whisper of the Lord's still small voice? God was not in the wind, earthquake, or fire for Elijah; rather, God spoke in a "gentle whisper," sometimes translated "still small voice" or "sheer silence." (1Kings 19:11-16) Through God's word and many of those time-tested "practices or disciplines," Jesus' Spirit inside of you will speak to you in a gentle whisper. Inspiring the still small voice inside of you, the Holy Spirit will give you practical, specific and helpful guidance.

Hearing the Lord's gentle whisper is very exciting. It always has a definite sense of being initiated by God. I say to myself, *"Wow! I didn't make that up."* Amazingly the Lord's whisper always seems to be "gentle" no matter what.

We live in a "noisy" world. In order to hear Jesus speak, you will need to practice intentional "silence," quieting your mind, emotions and whatever else needs to be "quieted."

"Quiet" yourself with this exercise. It is not a rigid step-by-step process. Use whatever theme and variation works for you. Reflect using your imagination. Combine your contemplation with journaling, transcribing your thoughts. For more on journaling, refer to the final section of this chapter. Rather than pretending or hiding your true thoughts and feelings, journaling can assist and even force you to honestly reveal them to God. Transparency with the living God leads to grace and mercy.

1. Surrender all anxiety, tension, and troublesome emotions. Offer these to your Heavenly Father. Pray like this: *"Lord, I surrender all my troubles to you… my anxiety about my presentation at work, the tension I am feeling with my father…"*
2. Surrender control of your life. If you have trouble, picture Jesus before you, perhaps on the cross. Concentrate on Him.
3. Surrender all of your cares and worries. Place them one by one in a box. Then hand the box to your Heavenly Father.

4. Surrender all your good intentions. Instead, Jesus will give you His good intentions.

5. Surrender your sin and failures, confessing them and turning from them.

6. Now fill your thoughts with one of God's promises (see Appendix D).

7. Receive Jesus' unending forgiveness given and accomplished for you when He died on the cross and rose to new life.

"Cease striving and know that I am God!" Psalm 46:10 NASB

Second Challenge: Pray the Scriptures

"Praying Scripture," sometimes called *lectio divina* (translated as "divine reading"), is a common way the living God gently whispers. This type of meditative prayer has much theme and variation. Here is a variation:

1. Choose a short passage of Scripture, perhaps a few words or a verse. A wonderful list of the Lord's promises from Scripture is found in Appendix D. Here is a suggestion:

"Come to me, all you who are weary and burdened, and I will give you rest. Take my yoke upon you and learn from me, for I am gentle and humble in heart, and you will find rest for your souls. For my yoke is easy and my burden is light." Matthew 11:28-30

2. Picture Jesus with you. Thank Him for His presence. Invite Him to speak to you.

3. Read the Scripture very slowly, one word at a time. Stay with each word until you believe the Lord is moving you to the next. You might stay with one word the entire time.
4. Pay attention to your thoughts. This may be Jesus speaking to you, perhaps guiding, healing or teaching.
5. Talk to Jesus as you read. Pray, using the words from Scripture.
6. Jot down your thoughts: a word, a few sentences or whatever seems appropriate. Maybe write a poem or prayer, draw, paint or use some other creative way to express your thoughts.
7. Respond to the Lord with whatever comes from your heart. Thank Him for speaking.
8. If needed, discuss your experience with a respected and trustworthy companion.
9. Remember receiving Jesus' guidance is not according to your agenda. Listening is not about quantity rather quality and depth.

What did Jesus say to you?

_____

_____

_____

As you listen, exercise creativity and freedom, remembering that the Lord guides in many ways. Expect different seasons. Sometimes your experience will seem like a desert. Other times you will visit the mountaintop. Sometimes you will sense you are to wait. Remember Jesus is all about calling you, speaking, guiding, and giving vision. His guidance will always be on time, sometimes early, but never late. Pray these words:

"Your word is a lamp for my feet, a light on my path." Psalm 119:105

Third Challenge: Create Time and Space

When asked, *"How are you?"* … too many respond: *"busy!"* Intentionally creating time and space in order to listen for the Lord's gentle whisper is a great "get to do it," not a "have to do it." Time spent listening will not be wasted and unproductive; instead, it will be the opposite, increasing productivity. Schedule a retreat, or set aside a longer period of time—a Saturday morning, Sunday afternoon or time spent on an airplane. If it helps, have a place that facilitates listening. Intentionally "practice" solitude and real silence. Real silence—the absence of phones, computers or people talking to you—for a few hours or even days can enhance your ability to hear and recognize Jesus' voice. As you become familiar with His voice during these intentional times, you also will begin to recognize it at other times.

Once again for many, a little less TV or internet would create time for listening. How will you create time and space in order to listen for Jesus?

_____

_____

_____

Consider the pace of your life as you contemplate these words:

"Then, because so many people were coming and going that they did not even have a chance to eat, Jesus said to them, 'Come with me by yourselves to a quiet place and get some rest.' So they went away by themselves in a boat to a solitary place." Mark 6:31-32

Prayer: Richard Foster instructs how to create a personal "breath prayer:"

Set apart some uninterrupted time and find a quiet spot. In silence, allow the loving presence of God to surround you. After a bit, wait for God to call you by name: *"Arthur," "Scott," "Angie."* Wait for this question to come to mind: *"What do you want?"* Answer this question directly and simply. A word might pop into your mind: *"joy," "faith," "comfort."* Perhaps a phrase will surface: *"to feel your peace"* or *"to meaningfully be with you."* Next, connect this phrase with the most comfortable way you have of speaking about God: *"Gracious Lord" "Merciful Father" "God my Provider" "Awesome Savior" or "Light of the World."* Write out your breath prayer, saying only what is easily spoken in one breath. For example: *"Loving Jesus, personally speak with your awesome wisdom."* [4] In the cracks and spaces throughout your day, use your breath prayer to talk to Jesus. Continually, it will remind you that you are enfolded by His loving and constant presence.

Further Thoughts and Actions

- **Study the companion volume, *Custom Designed: A Life Worthy of the Call*.** For real life illustrations and to develop added insight, examine the corresponding chapter.

- **Use the Bible as a guidebook for your life.** When you feel worried or challenged, read and meditate upon a scripture verse or two. Use a concordance (Biblical index) to locate passages with a word pertaining to your life circumstances such as "anxious" or "encouragement." Allow the Lord to speak to you through these life-giving words, bringing hope, transforming your outlook or showing you some new step of action. If reading Scripture is new to you, begin with a Gospel or in the New Testament. The Lord's living active word will transform you. (Isaiah 55:10-11, Hebrews 4:12-16)

- **Consider journaling.** Do not make journaling into a hard exercise. Write in your journal when it works for you, even if very sporadically. Track your thoughts, ideas, impressions, fears and all of what the Lord reveals to you.

Long ago, I began keeping a prayer journal. I never dreamed that I would still be at it years later. By prayer journal, I am not talking about a list of prayer concerns—though this also is a helpful type of prayer journal. In the early days of journaling, I wrote letters to God, expressing what was happening with me: my thoughts, feelings, concerns, joys, blessings, sinfulness, worries, cares, concerns or desires. Sometimes I would describe a difficult situation or confess my failures and wrongs, seeking Jesus' mercy and forgiveness. Sometimes I might write how Jesus had encouraged me. I wrote with the expectation that the living God was reading all that I wrote.

Sometimes in response, I would wait for the Lord to write a letter back to me. I would write: *"Dear Wendy...,"* and then low and behold, sometimes a whole stream of first person thoughts would be inspired within me, something like the following: *"I love you, my child. You are precious to me. I am working through this circumstance. Wait for me to work in this situation."* The Lord has spoken many and various personal and practical words to me. Now most of the time, I do not write letters. Rather I use shorthand, writing a few words or thoughts. Spiritual journaling is one of the many time-tested practices through which the Lord may speak to you.

- Try ***Practicing the Presence of God***. Brother Lawrence, a monk of the historical church wrote a well-known book with this title. "Practicing the presence of God" is a very useful "practice" for "busy" persons. "Practice the presence of God" in all the activities of your day with a joyful awareness of God's presence, whispering prayers of praise and adoration as they continually flow from your heart. Breath prayers can assist in practicing the presence of God. Brother Lawrence knew the tranquility of God equally in the time of prayer as in the time of business.

- **Speak to Jesus using the "Jesus Prayer,"** a breath prayer from Scripture. Throughout your day, use the rhythm of your breathing to pray over and over, *"Lord Jesus, Son of God, have mercy on me, a sinner."* Add more meaning by prayerfully reflecting upon the scripture passage where this prayer originates (Luke 18:9-14).

- **Read a book on God's guidance.** Here is a suggestion:
  Hearing God by Dallas Willard

- **Random Thoughts:** Record any thoughts, feelings, ideas or actions that come to you.

CHAPTER 7
CALLED TO SUPPORT AND TRUST

The Lord is Calling: Matthew 18:20; Acts 2:1, 42-47; Acts 13:1-3; Ephesians 4:15-16; Colossians 3:12-17; Hebrews 10:24-45; 1 Thessalonians 5:11

You won't be able to go it alone. Jesus called a group of disciples who together followed Him. Later Jesus sent these disciples out two by two. Jesus taught: *"For where two or three gather in my name, there am I with them."* (Matthew 18:20) After Jesus ascended to the Father, the early Christians were "all together." (Acts 2:1, 42-47) The Holy Spirit called Paul and Barnabus in the midst of the church, the called out ones (plural):

"Now in the church at Antioch there were prophets and teachers: Barnabas, Simeon called Niger, Lucius … Manaen... and Saul. While they were worshiping the Lord and fasting, the Holy Spirit said, "Set apart for me Barnabas and Saul for the work to which I have called them." So after they had fasted and prayed, they placed their hands on them and sent them off." Acts 13:1-3

Thankfully the Lord is still alive, speaking and calling through the Holy Spirit present in His body—His people. If you don't already, you also need to "gather" and be "together" regularly with other followers of Jesus. Otherwise you will begin to drift and fall away from Jesus. *"Koininia"* as summarized in Chapter 5 is an apt description for the kind of relationships you will need. Trustworthy, respected and faith-filled friends and family will help you to discern your call. These people will clarify the guidance that you receive. Their support will encourage you to persevere and stay focused. They also will function as a check and balance, keeping you on track to live worthy of Jesus and His call (Observe the center of Diagram A in Chapter 1).

So, let's intentionally consider who will be your team of "call" companions, discerning, supporting and praying for you. Not all the people who care about you can assume this role. First, you will need people who are prayerful with significant spiritual insight, wisdom, and knowledge of the Scriptures. All guidance and resulting action needs to be formed by the Scriptures, not conflicting with their teaching. Second, good spiritual companions will not only care about you, but also know you and the quality of your faith. Their knowledge of both you and Scripture will provide needed perspective to listen and also weigh what you believe God is saying and calling you to do.

Trust and trustworthiness are prerequisites for your team. Trustworthy people wait to be invited into someone's life. They are all about listening and understanding another's thoughts and emotions. They generously offer encouragement (inner courage), and a positive, though realistic view of things. They are very safe confidantes, guarding your secrets. They understand relationship boundaries, never pressuring anyone to share outside of their personal comfort zone; rather, they understand the honor of being entrusted with another's true inner feelings and thoughts.

Trustworthy family and friends offer advice and critique sparingly, usually waiting to be asked for their feedback. When they offer critique, they speak respectfully without personal attack and "you" language. They view their own assessment with hesitation, knowing that they do not have God and life all figured out. They rarely offer easy answers for complex life situations.

Trustworthy people do not have an over inflated view of themselves. Instead most of the time (though not all the time), they have an honest, accurate view of themselves, both positive and negative. As appropriate, they are willing to be transparent—revealing a true representation of themselves; thus, pretense is minimal.

Waiting for affirmation from those who have a natural leadership role in your life—your parents, work supervisor, or church leaders—is a very easy way to test supposed guidance, whether it truly is from God ... especially if the guidance has implications for others under these leaders' care.

Even if they do not have an active relationship with the living God, your spouse or parents (if they still financially support you) should be included in your discernment process unless you are unsafe (Then, you should seek help). Though some parents and spouses may be too close to a situation, still God will use them.

The Biblical Greek word for the Holy Spirit used in John 14-16 literally means "called-alongside-one." It is translated in many and various ways: Encourager, Comforter, Counselor, Advocate, Helper, Intercessor, Strengthener, and Standby. Though only the living God has all these attributes, interestingly they describe well an ideal and trustworthy "call" companion.

"And let us consider how we may spur one another on toward love and good deeds, not giving up meeting together, as some are in the habit of doing, but encouraging one another—and all the more as you see the Day approaching." Hebrews 10:24-25

First Challenge: Identify Your Team

What family and friends have been your genuine, loyal and loving cheerleaders?

_____

_____

_____

Who do you deeply respect for their insight and wisdom, especially spiritual insight and wisdom?

_____

_____

_____

To whom could you bare your soul, sharing your true thoughts and feelings?

_____

_____

_____

Who does or might pray for you consistently and regularly?

_____

_____

_____

Who encourages you to grow in a loving, non-threatening, affirming and even healing way?

_____

_____

_____

Who do you feel comfortable asking for feedback and advice?

_____

_____

_____

Who might have potential to be on your support team if you were to develop a deeper relationship? Why?

_____

_____

_____

You will need a team who collectively has all these characteristics. Maybe you have a pastor, spiritual director or even a professional counselor who in some way has many of them. Bear in mind however that for various reasons, not all friends, pastors, spiritual directors or professional counselors can be your "call" companion. It is not wrong to conclude this.

"Therefore encourage one another and build each other up, just as in fact you are doing." 1 Thessalonians 5:11

Second Challenge: Seek Reliable Counsel

Go to one of your "call" companions and seek reliable counsel. Reflect and pray about what you will discuss with them … perhaps a challenge or section from this guide. What rises to the surface or feels like a mystery? If you feel comfortable, intentionally ask for feedback and advice. Ask him or her to pray with you. Ask for prayer on an ongoing basis. Jot down ideas for your conversation.

_____

_____

_____

Did you learn anything? Was this person able to offer good insight? Why or why not? Would you seek this person's counsel again? Why or why not?

_____

_____

_____

Consider talking to someone else as well. Invest in finding trustworthy "call" companions that you respect.

> *"Better a poor but wise youth than an old but foolish king who no longer knows how to take warning." Ecclesiastes 4:13*

Prayer: Pray for each person on your "team." Ask the Lord to bless them. Specifically thank the Lord for how each one has positively influenced your life. Ask God to mold and shape you into a "trustworthy and respected" friend.

Further Thoughts and Actions

- **Study the companion volume, *Custom Designed: A Life Worthy of the Call*.** For real life illustrations and to develop added insight, examine the corresponding chapter.

- **Try a Group:** Try a group where you can develop your relationship with Jesus, discern your call and also develop deeper friendships… perhaps a Bible study or spiritual growth group. Perhaps you need a focus group that shares common interests with you. Maybe gather a group, hand picking and inviting others to the group. If a group does not fit you, you can always quit. You shouldn't feel compelled to stay in a group where you feel uncomfortable, or your time is not well spent. With groups, there are no guarantees.

- **Random Thoughts:** Record any thoughts, feelings, ideas or actions that come to you.

THE PURPOSE

TRANSFORM THE WORLD ... YOUR UNIQUE PART!

Jesus is calling you! Jesus has given His "power" and prepared the "places" so that you can partner in His "plan," accomplishing the Father's "purposes."

Jesus was called to make the rule and reign of God available to others, proclaiming and demonstrating the Father's purposes. Jesus encouraged continual repentance, a great invitation to positive, real and significant change. At the beginning of his ministry and from that time on, Jesus began to proclaim:

"Repent, for the kingdom of heaven has come near." Matthew 4:17

The kingdom of heaven is not merely a future destination, but it is wherever the living God is ruling and reigning right here and right now. Whenever and wherever the Lord is ruling and reigning, transformation is happening: Bondage becomes freedom. Darkness becomes light. Blindness becomes sight. Death becomes life. Bad news becomes good news!

From the Hebrew Scriptures, the *"Mikra,"* (translated "calling"), Jesus heard and discerned His Father "calling." After Jesus was "anointed" with the Holy Spirit's power, He returned to His hometown and announced His "calling" from the *"Mikra:"*

"The scroll of the prophet Isaiah was handed to him. Unrolling it, he found the place where it is written: 'The Spirit of the Lord is upon me, because he has anointed me

to bring good news to the poor. He has sent me to proclaim release to the captives and recovery of sight to the blind, to set the oppressed free, to proclaim the year of the Lord's favor'… He began by saying to them, 'Today this scripture is fulfilled in your hearing.'" Luke 4:17-19, 21 from Isaiah 61:1-2

Beginning with Jesus' temptation by Satan all the way to the cross, Jesus proclaimed God's heavenly rule and reign, ushering in the great reversal of sin, death and evil. Jesus was a problem breaker, confronting, forgiving, transforming, healing and conquering every form of sin, death and evil with God's heavenly rule and reign. Jesus was a goodness maker, magnifying and multiplying the Lord's steadfast love, presence, grace and glory. Jesus taught that the kingdom of heaven is like a small amount of yeast, leavening an entire loaf. Sometimes He "looked up to heaven," and then demonstrated the power of the kingdom of heaven with an incredible miracle.

From the start of his ministry all the way to the cross, Jesus challenged sin, death, evil and the power of the devil. Jesus was so "passionate" about the Father's purposes He was willing to suffer for His "passion." Jesus suffered the consequences for sin, paying for freedom with His own life and blood; however, His Father resurrected Him from the dead. The resurrection proclaims that sin, death, evil and the power of the devil will not have the final word.

Jesus called and partnered with His disciples—apprentices—teaching, training and imitating for them how to participate in the great reversal of sin, death, evil and the power of the devil. Jesus is still alive, present and partnering with ordinary people like you to recreate reform and renew people, places and problems with God's rule, reign and resurrection power. Jesus is calling!

The world still needs a voice in the wilderness, light in the darkness, and the healing and freedom that reverse and triumph over every form of brokenness and bondage. Jesus is still alive through the resurrection, ruling, reigning and proclaiming: *"I have died for you. Your sins are forgiven. Evil and death in all of their many manifestations have been defeated. I will save, heal and set you free!"*

Ordinary people called by Jesus and anointed with the Holy Spirit's power in order to transform people, places and problems ... this is the living God's plan and purpose! It's also real church! Remember "Christian church" in the Biblical Greek literally means *"anointed and called-out-ones."* You are the church, "called out" by Jesus to participate in His ongoing transformation of the world. Being a "member" of the church, the called out ones, is not a name on a list; rather, a "member" as described in Scripture is a body part. Being a "member" is having a unique and significant part and function in Jesus' ongoing kingdom purposes still happening today through His people—His body. You're an important part of Christ Jesus' body (1 Corinthians 12). Do you know your unique part in Jesus' kingdom purposes? How are you "called out" by Jesus to transform the world?

The Purpose

Proclaim and demonstrate the kingdom of heaven! Transform the world! Know your unique part!

Chapter 8 Called to the Great Reversal

CHAPTER 8
CALLED TO THE GREAT REVERSAL

The Lord is Calling: Ecclesiastes 3:11; Mark 1:15-16; Luke 4:1-19; Matthew 4:1-25; 5:1-7:29; Matthew 13:1-58

God has set eternity in our hearts (Ecclesiastes 3:11). Not only do we long for eternity in the future, but we are called to have an influence and impact now that will last throughout eternity. The Lord has wired within you an important part of His eternal and heavenly vision. Jesus is calling you to passionately participate in His purposes. Jesus taught His disciples how to converse with His Heavenly Father, praying for His heavenly purposes:

"This, then, is how you should pray: 'Our Father in heaven, holy be your name, your kingdom come, your will be done, on earth as it is in heaven. Give us today our daily bread. And forgive us our debts, as we also have forgiven our debtors. And lead us not into temptation, but deliver us from the evil one.'" Matthew 6:9-13

Not only do these words teach us how to pray, they also outline Jesus' agenda and kingdom purposes.

"Your kingdom come, your will be done on earth as it is in heaven." Not only did Jesus pray for the kingdom to come, He also proclaimed and demonstrated

the kingdom of heaven was near and here and now with all its power. Jesus is calling you to the same.

What is your important part in the Lord's heavenly vision? How will His *"kingdom come on earth as in heaven"* through you? Though you may not realize it, having a heavenly vision will uncover what you're called to say and do now. A heavenly vision will change your expectations of what Jesus can accomplish for you and through you right now. Although it is difficult to explain how this happens, having a heavenly vision will shed light on the passions and burdens for the world that God has purposed and planted within you. Below is a heavenly vision to help you understand. It is based upon Scripture and a sermon I once heard: [5]

Heaven will be the very best of the best. Streets will be paved in gold, and all things will be made of the finest things. The extraordinary beauty of God will be all around: the greatest mountains, the most extraordinary gardens, the bluest clearest rivers and lakes, and forests filled with exquisite fall color. The light of God's glory will shine continually.

Heaven will have the greatest intellect and creativity. In heaven, each of us will learn from all the very best masters of all time: the greatest musicians, crafts people, artists, thinkers, writers, scholars, inventors, and athletes. If you're lacking competence in any of these things, you will acquire it in heaven.

Heaven will be the most fun party and very best celebration ever. Fun in heaven will exceed whatever fun you already have experienced.

Heaven will be a place of great reversals. Heaven will be everything good and right. Boredom will be reversed and replaced by true fulfillment, purpose and meaning. Love will replace hate. The great "yes" of God will replace critique. Laughter will replace tears. Happiness will replace sadness. Joy will replace mourning and travail. Peaceful relationships characterized by true, loyal and authentic friendship will replace hurt, falsehood, pretense, enmity, conflict and war. Health, wholeness, equality and justice will replace brokenness, sickness, and poverty. Evil will be reversed and replaced by everlasting good.

In heaven, you will share in the greatest most fulfilling and uninterrupted friendship with Jesus. You will know the Lord's profound love. As a result, God's values and character will be honored and desired by all. Now this is not the real heavenly vision. Heaven will be much better (1 Corinthians 2:9).

Remember "heaven" is not only a place we anticipate in the future, but the kingdom of heaven is wherever Jesus is ruling and reigning right here and right now. Day by day, Jesus transformed people, places and problems, announcing and demonstrating the availability of the kingdom of heaven: *"Blessed are the poor in spirit, for theirs is the kingdom of heaven. Blessed are those who…"* (Matthew 5:3-4) Jesus was a problem breaker, forgiving and reversing every form of sin, death and evil. He was a goodness maker, multiplying and magnifying the glory of God.

Is Jesus ruling and reigning in you? If so, the kingdom of heaven is within you. Jesus is calling you to make the kingdom of heaven available to others, reversing every form of sin, death and evil while multiplying God's goodness, grace and glory. In this world, there are a multitude of needs! May Jesus plant His purposeful passion within you! You're an important part of God's "heavenly" vision for this world! You have a "heavenly call!"

"I press on toward the goal for the prize of the heavenly call of God in Christ Jesus." Philippians 3:14 NRSV

First Challenge: Your Passions and Burdens?

What has Jesus done for you? How has Jesus transformed you? How could you tell others about what He has done for you? Jot down significant experiences, moments and people. Sometime, record your entire life and history with Jesus.

———————————————————————————————

———————————————————————————————

———————————————————————————————

Contemplate each part of Jesus' prayer: *"Our Father in heaven, holy be your name, your kingdom come, your will be done, on earth as it is in heaven. Give us today our daily bread. And forgive us our debts, as we also have forgiven our debtors. And lead us not into temptation, but deliver us from the evil one."* Examine and reflect upon each part of the prayer. What is Jesus saying to you? What are you called to do?

———————————————————————————————

———————————————————————————————

———————————————————————————————

Contemplate the heavenly vision described above. What is most attractive, intriguing, motivational, energizing, exciting or fun for you? What would you add to this heavenly vision?

———————————————————————————————

———————————————————————————————

———————————————————————————————

"Your kingdom come, your will be done, on earth as it is in heaven." As you consider this heavenly vision, how can God's "kingdom come on earth as it is in heaven" through you? What are you called to do? How can you be a problem breaker and goodness maker? What problems would you most like to solve? Who and what could you transform? How can you train and equip others to do the same?

_____

_____

_____

Ideally, as you imagine a perfect world, what would this look like to you?" What comes to mind first? What would it look like if the Lord was reigning in every person and place?

_____

_____

_____

Reflect on these words: *"So if anyone is in Christ, there is a new creation: everything old has passed away; see everything has become new!"* (2 Corinthians 5:17 NRSV) What is the Lord saying to you?

_____

_____

_____

Summarize your responses in this challenge. What are your passions? What are your burdens for the world? How could God's heavenly vision become reality in your work, family, church, neighborhood, community and world … both now and in the future?

_____

_____

_____

Reflect upon these inspiring words that are true for you:

"What no eye has seen, nor ear heard, nor the human heart conceived, what God has prepared for those who love him'—these things God has revealed to us through the Spirit;" 1 Corinthians 2:9 NRSV

Second Challenge: Consider Extraordinary People

Through word and deed, great people of God, past and present, have demonstrated the availability of the kingdom of heaven. Like you, all of these people were ordinary people. Study extraordinary people from Scripture and throughout history including today. Read biographies or listen to testimonials of saints, martyrs or other faithful people. Ponder their lives and imitate their ways, considering what made them extraordinary. Research someone who shares similar interests with you. Who could you study?

_____

_____

_____

Who have been extraordinary and inspirational people for you? Consider both people you have learned about and also people you have personally known. What made these people extraordinary and inspiring? How could you imitate their ways? What could you learn from their example? God desires for you to be extraordinary ... do you believe this? Why or why not? How can you become extraordinary?

_____

_____

_____

God desires to give you heavenly hope:

"See the home of God is among mortals. He will dwell with them; they will be his peoples, and God himself will be with them; he will wipe every tear from their eyes. Death will be no more; mourning and crying and pain will be no more, for the first things have passed away." Revelation 21:3-7 NRSV

Prayer

"Our Father who is in heaven, holy is your name. Your kingdom come, your will be done on earth as it is in heaven. Give us this day our daily bread. Forgive us our sins as we forgive those who sin against us. Lead us not into temptation, but deliver us from the evil one. For to you belongs the kingdom, the power and the glory forever and ever. AMEN"

Further Thoughts and Actions

- Study the companion volume, *Custom Designed: A Life Worthy of the Call.* For real-life illustrations and to develop added insight, examine the corresponding chapter.

- **Create a Personal Mission Statement(s):** Similar to a corporation or church, write a personal mission statement. A mission statement can focus your life. Perhaps write different mission statements for your work, family, your part in your church gathering, and your neighborhood, community and world.

- **Random Thoughts:** Record any thoughts, feelings, ideas or actions that come to you.

PRESS ON TO WIN THE RACE!

"Press on" is race language. The apostle Paul encouraged the early Christians and now you to "press on," pursuing Jesus' call as if you wanted to win a race:

"Not that I have already obtained all this, or have already arrived at my goal, but I press on to take hold of that for which Christ Jesus took hold of me. Brothers and sisters, I do not consider myself yet to have taken hold of it. But one thing I do: Forgetting what is behind and straining toward what is ahead, I press on toward the goal to win the prize for which God has called me heavenward in Christ Jesus." Philippians 3:12-14

Press on! So, what makes an Olympic racer successful? A racer needs training and practice, clear priorities, a proper diet, a plan, perseverance, persistence, an intentional pattern of life, and partners to encourage and support. Much of the same will help you to "win the prize," living worthy of Jesus and His call. The apostle Paul knew this:

"But whatever were gains to me I now consider loss for the sake of Christ. What is more, I consider everything a loss because of the surpassing worth of knowing Christ Jesus my Lord, for whose sake I have lost all things. I consider them garbage, that I may gain Christ and be found in him…" Philippians 3:7-9

Paul knew that he needed to "forget what is behind." He needed to put his "gains" in proper perspective so that they would not distract and detour him from Jesus' call. Worldly "gains" such as prestige, human power, popularity, and wealth can detour us from the Lord's call. Likewise, regret, guilt and brokenness can distract us as well. Ultimately, Satan the evil one will deceive and detour, using whatever and whomever—even if seemingly good. Satan steals and destroys, turning people away from Jesus and His kingdom call (Ephesians 6:10-13). After His baptism, the devil tried to tempt Jesus from His Father's plan and purpose; however, Jesus "pressed on." Jesus continued to press on in spite of rejection (even in His hometown), and having no pillow of his own.

Jesus told a parable about planting and growing seeds. He used seeds to illustrate how Satan and the cares of life ultimately diminish kingdom fruitfulness. Some hear God's word, producing little fruit due to the devil and distractions of life. Still others hear God's word and it takes root, leading to fruit a hundredfold. (Mark 4:1-20)

Do you feel as if you are forever detoured from what is most important, especially Jesus and His call? It's time to get serious so that you can "press on" to win the prize! How can you live worthy of Jesus and His call, running the race like an Olympic athlete? Let's press on!

Press On!

Pursue Jesus' call! Train and practice! Set priorities! Wisely use your time and resources! Persevere! Increase your confidence! Create an intentional pattern of life! Win the race!

CHAPTER 9
CALLED TO TAKE STEPS AND WALK

The Lord is Calling: Psalm 37:5; Luke 8:1-21; Luke 9:21-26; Romans 12:1-2; Ephesians 2:8-10; Ephesians 3:20-4:10; Ephesians 5:15-20; Colossians 1:9-14

It's time to get moving!

*"Now to him who is able to do immeasurably more than all we ask or imagine, according to his power that is at work within us, to him be glory in the called out ones and in Christ Jesus throughout all generations, forever and ever! Amen. Therefore, as a prisoner for the Lord, I am earnestly calling you to walk **in conformity** with the calling to which you were called." Ephesians 3:20-4:1 Author's translation*

Here "in conformity" is translated from the Biblical Greek word, *axios,* more often translated "worthy." *Axios* can refer to a balance-scale, which uses weights to create equilibrium, thus weighing an object and determining its worth. Here the apostle Paul is saying: Jesus called you, now walk "in conformity" or "in balance" with the worth and weightiness of His call.

Are you living "worthy" of Jesus and "in balance" with His call? Jesus has called you to partner in His purposeful plan, knowing, following and serving Him. The Lord has anointed you, pouring out His Spirit, giving you His power, spiritual gifts and other unique attributes. Jesus has prepared the places of your unique mission field: family, work, neighborhood, community and church gathering. Jesus is calling!

So, what's next? Perhaps this is overwhelming or you're not sure where to start. Is life already too complicated? If so, take my friend's advice: *"Don't worry so much about these things. Don't even think about them. Instead, make it your No. 1 goal in life to know Jesus and then all else will fall into place."* This is where to begin! This goal will be sufficient!

Next, ask Jesus to take control and be in charge! Surrender to Him, allowing Him to be "Lord." Offer your unique gifts, attributes, resources, plans ... your entire life to Jesus who deeply loves you. (Romans 12:1-2) Wait for Him to show the way!

Be hopeful! Someday you will wake up, suddenly realizing that Jesus has put the pieces together. You're walking and even running in conformity with the Lord's call, pressing on to win the race! Then offer praise and thanksgiving to Jesus! So, let's press on!

"The one who calls you is faithful, and he
will do this." 1 Thessalonians 5:24 NRSV

First Challenge: Assess Your Progress

Knowing Jesus ... is this your No. 1 goal in life? Are you willing to offer all of your life to the Lord, following wherever Jesus leads and whatever it takes? Why or why not? Ask Jesus to make you willing to be willing.

_____

_____

_____

Contemplate those "P" words: power, place, plan and purpose. How is the Holy Spirit and "power" at work in you? What are your spiritual gifts? What are other significant attributes of your personal profile? What are the "places" of your unique mission field? What is your important part in the Lord's "plan and purposes?" "Who are you?" "What are you supposed to do?" Try summarizing your responses with another "elevator speech" (Elevator speech? See Chapter 3, Challenge 7 and Chapter 4, Challenge 3).

_____

_____

_____

The Lord is speaking these important words to you:

"Therefore, I urge you, brothers and sisters, in view of God's mercy, to offer your bodies as a living sacrifice, holy and pleasing to God—this is your true and proper worship. Do not conform to the pattern of this world, but be transformed by the renewing of your mind. Then you will be able to test and approve what God's will is—his good, pleasing and perfect will." Romans 12:1-2

Second Challenge: Increase Your Effectiveness

Several factors can either facilitate or hinder your ability to live worthy of Jesus and His call. Study the issues represented in this equation:

Living in Conformity with Jesus' Call

=

Relationship with Jesus + Unique Profile + Spiritual Gifts + Guidance + "Call" Companions + Time + Money + Confidence + Training

What aspects of the equation are weak, missing or a mystery? Why? What does this equation suggest to you?

_____

_____

_____

Have patience and wait for the Lord. Let these words assure you:

"The Lord is my light and my salvation; whom shall I fear? ...I believe that I shall see the goodness of the LORD in the land of the living. Wait for the LORD; be strong, and let your heart take courage; wait for the LORD!" Psalm 27:1, 13-14 NRSV

Third Challenge: Identify Steps

Check whatever steps might be helpful to you:

_____ Review and reflect upon my unique attributes and individuality. (Chapter 2)

_____ Clarify and understand my spiritual gifts. (Chapter 3)

_____ Experiment with my spiritual gifts. Seek opportunities to use them. (Chapter 3)

_____ Identify the places of my unique mission field. Develop a vision for these places. (Chapter 4)

_____ Sharpen my focus and purpose by clearly discerning my passions and burdens for the world. (Chapter 8)

_____ Strengthen my relationship with Jesus, making it the greatest of all relationships. (Chapter 5)

_____ Develop my ability to hear Jesus' voice and discern His guidance. (Chapter 6)

_____ Seek reliable counsel from trustworthy people. (Chapter 7)

Based upon what you have checked, what do you need to do next?

_____

_____

_____

Identify some needs. Check all statements that apply to you:

_____ I don't have time. I'm already too busy. (Chapters 10 & 12)

_____ I feel trapped or locked into my current lifestyle. (Chapter 10)

_____ I like my lifestyle and am afraid that I might be asked to sacrifice. (Chapter 10)

_____ I need confidence to move ahead. (Chapter 11)

_____ I need encouragement to move ahead. (Chapters 7 & 11)

_____ I feel hampered by my weaknesses. (Chapter 11)

_____ I feel trapped by regrets. (Chapter 11)

_____ Fear and other mental hurdles seem always in the way. (Chapter 11)

_____ I am not sure that I have everything it takes to move ahead. (Chapter 11)

_____ I feel inadequate for the task. (Chapter 11)

_____ I need to be better equipped with more training, skill or experience. (Chapter 11)

_____ I feel overwhelmed and do not know where to start. (Chapters 5, 10 & 12)

_____ I need to integrate all the pieces. (Chapter 12)

_____ I need help. (Chapters 5, 6 & 7)

Based upon what you have checked, what do you need to do next? How would you summarize what you have checked?

_____

_____

_____

Daily ask Jesus: *"Lord, what are you saying to me?"* Invite Him to show you what to do today. Listen for His guidance, focusing on today. Put His guidance into "practice." Today, this is Jesus' call for you. Then tomorrow, do the same. Have a long-term view. Be assured by these words:

"Strive first for the kingdom of God and his righteousness, and all these things will be given to you as well. So do not worry about tomorrow, for tomorrow will bring worries of its own. Today's trouble is enough for today." Matthew 6:33-34 NRSV

Fourth Challenge: Take Steps

What steps have you identified already?

_____

_____

_____

Additional steps are outlined in Appendix E. Study these steps. For other possible steps, review the corresponding chapter in the companion book, *Custom Designed: A Life Worthy of the Call*. What steps capture your attention?

_____

_____

_____

Sample or experiment with ideas. Try them on. Do they fit? What is uncomfortable? Try something small to confirm whether these ideas fit you. Record your thoughts.

_____

_____

_____

As you seek to live worthy of Jesus and in conformity with His call, what hampers or hinders you? What are barriers, hurdles or obstacles? What are your present fears and concerns?

_____

_____

_____

Identify meaningful words from Scripture or other wisdom to help. Memorize them.

_____

_____

_____

What kind of help do you need? Who could you ask? It's a sign of strength to ask for help. Everyone needs help at one time or another. Seek reliable counsel from someone you trust and respect. Share your thoughts with this person. Solicit feedback and advice. Did you learn anything? See Chapter 7 if you are unsure who to ask.

_____

_____

_____

Summarize all the steps you will take to move ahead. When will these happen? Make a commitment. Ask God to reveal a wise strategy.

_____

_____

_____

Have patience and wait for the Lord to reveal wisdom. Be assured by these words:

"If any of you is lacking wisdom, ask God, who gives to all generously and ungrudgingly, and it will be given to you." James 1:5 NSRV

Prayer: Jesus already knows and understands what is going on with you. Picture Jesus with you right now, praying for you because He is (Hebrews 7:25). Converse with Him:

Lord Jesus, I thank you that you are with me right now. I surrender my life to you. Take control. You know and understand all of what I am thinking and feeling. Thank you that you are praying for me. I offer to you my anxieties and fears: _____. I offer to you all that I am thinking and feeling: _____. In your powerful name, AMEN

Continually attempt to focus on Jesus, surrendering to Him. Converse with Him about everything! When you are captured by fear and anxiety, picture Jesus on the cross or emerging from the empty tomb.

Further Thoughts and Actions

- **Review the many ideas** in the corresponding chapter of the companion volume, *Custom Designed: A Life Worthy of the Call.*

- **Random Thoughts:** Record any thoughts, ideas, feelings or actions that come to you.

CHAPTER 10
CALLED TO A WISE ECONOMY OF LIFE

The Lord is Calling: Deuteronomy 8:1-20; Psalm 23; Ecclesiastes 2:22-26; Malachi 3:8-12; Matthew 6:19-34; 25:14-30; Mark 2:23-28; 10:17-31; Luke 12:13-48; Luke 21:1-4; Acts 2:40-47; 4:32-37; Philippians 4:6-14; 1 Timothy 6:6-19

Either Jesus' call can determine how you distribute your time, money and resources, or your time and resource "spending choices" can detour you from His call. The apostle Paul knew a significant secret:

"I have learned to be content whatever the circumstances. I know what it is to be in need, and I know what it is to have plenty. I have learned the secret of being content in any and every situation, whether well-fed or hungry, whether living in plenty or in want. I can do everything through him who gives me strength." Philippians 4:11b-13

Do you feel "content in any and every situation?" Perhaps instead, you feel trapped, restless or frustrated. Maybe you're not living in conformity with the Lord's call. Living worthy of Jesus and His call may seem like an unattainable and impossible luxury. Perhaps you're deep in debt, or you're bustling and "busy."

Using your time and resources is simply a series of choices. Do you make wise choices? Scripture outlines the wise and powerful principles of God's economy. "Practicing" the principles of God's economy will enable freedom and create contentment. Let's press on!

"Happy is everyone who fears the LORD, who walks in his ways. You shall eat the fruit of the labor of your hand; you shall be happy, and it shall go well with you… Thus shall the man be blessed who fears the LORD." Psalm 128:1-2, 4 NRSV

First Challenge: Who Gives the "Goods?"

God has entrusted many "goods" of life to you (Deuteronomy 8:1-12). What has God entrusted to you? Make a list of your "goods," recording not only material "goods" but also every nonmaterial "good."

_____

_____

_____

Your "goods" of life likely include: salvation, identity in Christ, call and purpose for living, family, friends, time, work, spiritual gifts, talents, skills, abilities, material resources, name, reputation, pleasure, food, clothing, shelter, water and the entire earth including its beauty. Who is the giver of these "goods?" How do you know this? How does this understanding affect the way you live?

_____

_____

_____

Do you tell yourself any of these lies?

- I am the maker and creator of my "goods."
- I am the owner of my "goods."
- I am the producer of my "goods."
- I am the creator of all my abilities to produce.
- I obtained my job.
- I am the creator of my time.

Which lies do you tell yourself? Why? Change your lies into truthful statements. For example, "God is the owner of all my 'goods, entrusting them to me.'"

_____

_____

_____

Reflect upon these truthful statements for a moment: *The Lord God is your provider. The Lord is the owner of your "goods."* How could these statements help you? How could they free you from worry and stress?

_____

_____

_____

Meditate on Jesus' words of promise:

"Therefore I tell you, do not worry about your life, what you will eat, or about your body, what you will wear. For life is more than food, and the body more than cloth-ing. Consider the ravens: they neither sow nor reap, they have neither storehouse nor barn and yet God feeds them. Of how much more value are you than the birds! And can any of you by worrying add a single hour to your span of life? If then

you are not able to do so small a thing as that, why do you worry about the rest? Consider the lilies, how they grow: they neither toil nor spin; yet I tell you, even Solomon in all his glory was not clothed like one of these. But if God so clothes the grass of the field, which is alive today and tomorrow is thrown into the oven, how much more will he clothe you—you of little faith! And do not keep striving for what you are to eat and what you are to drink, and do not keep worrying. For it is the nations of the world that strive after all these things, and your Father knows that you need them. Instead, strive for his kingdom, and these things will be given to you as well." Luke 12:22-31 NSRV

Second Challenge: Make Wise Choices

Poor priorities and choices challenge many people. Rather than joy and fulfillment, frustration, stress and restlessness result. Wise management leads to healthy and fruitful living.

Stewardship is a scriptural word, describing the wise management of all God's "goods." Thankfully stewardship is a personal lifestyle, not a program at church. It's the wise management of life… your life. From the Biblical Greek word for stewardship, we get our English word "economy." Stewardship is having a wise economy of life, practicing the principles of God's economy.

Time and money have a very helpful relationship in the "economy" of life. You can utilize time to make money, or you can use money to free up your time. So how could your time free up your money? In turn, how could money free up your time? Contemplate these words: *"living more with less."* Are they true? How could they be true for you? Discuss these issues with a trustworthy companion.

Jesus told a parable about a master *"going on a journey who called his servants and entrusted his property to them."* Each servant was entrusted with a different allotment of property to spend and manage. Upon his return, the Master or Lord asked for an accounting of His property. Two servants doubled their allotment. In turn, the Master gave more, doubling their allotment and rewarding their trustworthiness. The third servant buried his allotment, thus doing nothing. This servant "feared" that the Master was harsh and therefore, would take away his allotment. It could be asked how well the third servant knew the Master as his assessment does not match with how the Master treated the first two servants. Read Matthew 25:14-30.

Of course the Master is the Lord God. His property is all that the Lord has spoken into existence. God has entrusted you with an allotment of His property, your many "goods" of life. Unfortunately like the third servant, many fear the Master is harsh and will take away their allotment. Review your list of "goods" from the previous challenge. Which of these "goods" are you multiplying? Which of them are you "burying?" How are you "spending" your allotment of "goods?" How are you like the first two servants? How are you like the third servant? What kind of accounting will you give when the Lord returns, not only for your time and resources, but also your entire life?

Third Challenge: Distinguish Need and Want

Distinguishing between need and want enables wise choices. Needs are essential for life. Wants are everything else. What do you need for fullness of life? Include material and also non-material "goods" such as loyal friends and family.

_____

_____

_____

Your "needs" list probably includes: God, water, food, shelter, clothing, friends, family, salvation, the Lord's call and purpose for living, health and perhaps more. What are you lacking? Scripture teaches if you have more than you need, then you have abundance, and are rich. How are you rich? In contrast to Scripture, how do others define "rich?"

_____

_____

_____

How do the scriptural definitions of "need," "want," and "rich" create contentment and satisfaction? *"I need a new pair of jeans"* Do you ever tell yourself lies like this one? When and how often?

_____

_____

_____

God is the source, creator, owner and provider of all the "goods" of life. God promises to provide for our needs and sometimes even our wants:

"And my God will fully satisfy every need of yours according to his riches in glory in Christ Jesus." Philippians 4:19 NRSV

Fourth Challenge: Live Simply With Contentment

Unwise choices lead to overextension of both money and time. Overextension of money results in unwise debt. For example, carrying a large credit card balance is unwise debt, creating high payments while eliminating other spending choices; thus, freedom is limited, creating bondage and slavery. A similar bondage occurs with an overly full schedule.

Nearly always overextension is self-inflicted. Overextension is caused by an inability to wait or say "no." Stress, anxiety, frayed emotions, impatience, lack of rest, distance from God and an inability to relax, have fun, and positively engage in relationships are symptomatic of overextension.

Which symptoms of overextension are you currently experiencing? Describe the nature of overextension in your life. What changes could you make?

_____

_____

_____

Do you ever tell yourself any of these lies? Which ones? Why?

- "I have to have it now."
- "I have to do it now."
- "I will never get it for this price again."
- "I "need" it."

_____

_____

_____

Moderation is doing something a little less often or in a less expensive manner. For most, a less expensive car would be more than adequate. Self-discipline is saying "no" to yourself. Whether you are rich or poor, simplicity rests upon a simple fact: only the Lord brings contentment. With real contentment and wisdom, you can say "no," passing on all kinds of activity and stuff. You will also say "yes" at the appropriate times.

Remember the apostle Paul's "secret" expressed in Philippians 4:6-13. How will the "secret" of "contentment" affect how you "spend" time and money?

_____

_____

_____

Listen to these wise words of the Lord:

"But godliness with contentment is great gain. For we brought nothing into the world, and we can take nothing out of it. But if we have food and clothing, we will be content with that. Those who want to get rich fall into temptation and a trap and into many foolish and harmful desires that plunge people into ruin and destruction. For the love of money is a root of all kinds of evil. Some people, eager for money, have wandered from the faith and pierced themselves with many griefs." 1 Timothy 6:6-10

Fifth Challenge: Embrace Rest and Refreshment

God gave the Sabbath rest to protect people from overextension and anxiety. The Sabbath rest sustains through the week as it is remembered.

It also gives hope as its coming is anticipated. The Sabbath is not merely a rule, but rather a way of living. It is setting aside a day for the Lord and His values while ceasing from the week's routine activities. In turn, it's embracing all that brings holistic rest and refreshment. In order to rest and regain perspective, everyone needs to cease, enjoy, celebrate, receive, be refreshed, and be nourished by God's word and grace. Remember God created the Sabbath for humankind.

What activities and values fill up most of your week?

_____

_____

_____

What refreshes you? For you, what brings emotional, intellectual, spiritual and physical rest and refreshment? What brings enjoyment (inner joy)? What creates a contrast with the rest of your week? Which of these "refreshment" activities will you practice? If Sunday isn't possible, when will you practice the Sabbath rest for twenty-four hours out of your week?

_____

_____

_____

"Remember the Sabbath day and keep it holy." Remember "holy" means set apart for God. How will you set apart the Sabbath day for the Lord?

_____

_____

_____

The Sabbath was so important that the Lord included it in the "ten best ways to live," the "Ten Commandments."

"Remember the Sabbath day and keep it holy. Six days you shall labor and do all your work. But the seventh day is a Sabbath to the LORD your God; you shall not do any work—you, your son or your daughter, your male and female slave, your livestock, or the alien resident in your towns. For in six days the LORD made heaven and earth, the sea and all that is in them, but rested the seventh day; therefore the LORD blessed the Sabbath day and consecrated it." Exodus 20:8-11 NRSV

Sixth Challenge: Give Rather than Possess

Many times, possessions can possess and the love of money can lure (Luke 12:13-21). How do you feel "possessed" and "consumed" by possessions? How much time and money do you spend managing, maintaining and fixing all your possessions? How much time do you spend worrying about your money or possessions? How much time do you spend acquiring possessions (shopping)? Ultimately, how many of these possessions bring happiness and contentment?

_____

_____

_____

A false god is not merely a golden statue. Rather, it is anything you fear, love and trust more than the one true God. Your "spending" choices indicate the "first loves" of your life. Based upon how you "spend" your time and money, what are your "first loves?"

_____

_____

_____

Quite surprisingly, graciously giving away your money and possessions can set you free from the grip of greed. Wanting more is greed. Grace is the GREAT BIG EVERYTHING given to you by God. Jesus' grace can motivate natural, spontaneous, and cheerful giving (2 Corinthians 8 and 9). If you really know who gives the "goods," then you really do not need to "possess" them because they are not your own. Giving and investing in Jesus' work, and then seeing all the good that results, creates joy, freeing from greed, anxiety and false gods. Money and other resources can be a great tool for accomplishing the living God's eternal intentions.

How have you seen the Lord accomplish great things, using your money and other resources? How did you feel?

_____

_____

_____

Tithing is giving the first and best ten percent of the Lord's provision back to Him, and then trusting that He can provide for you with the rest—perhaps in ways unforeseen to you. If you truly believe that God provides all, then it will not be difficult to give the first and best ten percent of your provision. The Lord gave the tithe as a gift to protect His people from thinking that they were the makers and owners of their "goods." The Provider told His people:

> *"Will anyone rob God? Yet you are robbing me! But you say, 'How are we robbing you?' In your tithes and offerings! You are cursed with a curse, for you are robbing me—the whole nation of you! Bring the full tithe into the store house, so that there may be food in my house, and thus put me to the test, says the LORD of hosts; see if I will not open the windows of heaven for you and pour down for you an overflowing blessing." Malachi 3:8-10 NRSV*

What do you think of these words? What is your opinion of the tithe? If you were to give the first and best ten percent of your provision back to the Lord, how might He provide for you?

_____

_____

_____

When you offer your possessions to God, really you are offering yourself.

> *"I appeal to you therefore, brothers and sisters, by the mercies of God,*
> *to present your bodies as a living offering, holy and acceptable to God,*
> *which is your spiritual worship." Romans 12:1 NRSV*

Seventh Challenge: Share

Sharing is also a form of giving that creates greater versatility and freedom of choice. A group who "practices" their commonness in Jesus quite naturally will share with one another. Some may even co-own their possessions, holding them in "common." Sharing material, nonmaterial and spiritual "goods" between the materially and spiritually rich and poor will eliminate need, creating a just balance of life's "goods."

Brainstorm for a bit. Consider how you could more intentionally share your "goods." What could you comfortably make available to others? Who? How could you avoid buying things that you might borrow or co-own? Who has made you spiritually or relationally rich? Who has given you material resources? How have you experienced the joy of sharing? What projects could you accomplish with others? For example, groups of people have built barns together, both experiencing the joy of friendship and completing a needed task.

_____

_____

_____

Reflect upon the Lord's life-giving words:

"As for those who in the present age are rich, command them not to be haughty, or to set their hopes on the uncertainty of riches, but rather on God who richly provides us with everything for our enjoyment. They are to do good, to be rich in good works, generous, and ready to share, thus storing up for themselves the treasure of a good foundation for the future, so that they may take hold of the life that really is life." 1 Timothy 6:17-19 NRSV

Eighth Challenge: Rearrange Your Choices

Brainstorm and summarize how the principles of God's economy could positively and practically affect your "spending" choices. How could you rearrange your "spending" choices?

_____

_____

_____

How do your "spending" choices affect your ability to live worthy of Jesus and His call? How do they hinder? How do they facilitate? How could His call determine your "spending" choices?

_____

_____

_____

"All who believed were together and had all things in common; they would sell their possessions and goods and distribute the proceeds to all, as any had need. Day by day, as they spent much time together in the temple, they broke bread at home and ate their food with glad and generous hearts, praising God and having the good will of all the people. And day by day the Lord added to their number those who were being saved." Acts 2:44-47 NRSV

Prayer

"Merciful Lord, I offer with joy and thanksgiving what you have first given to me—myself, my time, and my possessions, signs of your gracious love. Receive them for the sake of him who offered himself for me, Jesus Christ my Lord. AMEN"[6]

Further Thoughts and Actions

- Study the companion volume, *Custom Designed: A Life Worthy of the Call*. For real life illustrations and to develop added insight, examine the corresponding chapter.

- **Write a note of thanks:** Who has shared their life or possessions with you?

- **Read** *Coat of Many Colors,* a children's book by Dolly Parton

- **Random Thoughts:** Record any thoughts, feelings, ideas or actions that come to you.

CHAPTER 11
CALLED TO CONFIDENCE AND FREEDOM

The Lord is Calling: Luke 22:31-46; John 10:10; John 14:1-16:33; Ephesians 6:10-20

Hearing Jesus' call may not be enough. Fear, inadequacy or a lack of confidence can steal, kill and destroy us. Jesus promised to provide what is needed to persevere and press ahead—in spite of discouragement, difficulties, setbacks and frustration. Just prior to His crucifixion, Jesus warned his disciples of the world's troubling trials while simultaneously promising encouragement. Jesus once dispersed and dissolved my discouragement with these words:

"I have told you these things, so that in me you may have peace. In this world you will have tribulation. But take courage! I have overcome the world." John 16:33 Author's translation

Jesus so unexpectedly and powerfully encouraged me that I could physically feel His presence. Following this experience, daily I began to record how the Lord appeared to me, encouraging me in the midst of ongoing difficult circumstances. Sometimes Scripture offered hope. Other times, I saw Jesus in an unexpected and positive occurrence. Upon occasion, a friend or family member spoke an uplifting word. Every so often I received

some surprise guidance or wisdom. Through these little and big epiphanies, I experienced Jesus' approval when human approval seemed absent.
I witnessed His living active presence in my life, encouraging, increasing
confidence and working against my hurt, fear, insecurity, discouragement
and difficult circumstances. "Encourage" means to give inner courage.

Jesus said, *"In this world you will have tribulation."* We can expect trials,
trouble and fear. Even the apostle Paul confessed to having *"fear and trem-*
bling" (1 Corinthians 2:3). Far too often, I'm the sinful problem maker,
creaming the confident, inflicting the innocent, or needlessly creating
chaos for myself. Sometimes difficulties come from another human who is
harming and hurting. Sometimes it's just because the world is broken and
unpredictable with accidents, tragedies, natural disasters and death.

Ultimately, Satan desires to destroy you, me and all others who trust in
Jesus because we are a part of the Lord's powerful plan. I have borne the
burden of hurtful relationships, rejection, sabotage, stage fright, cutting
critique, undermining, fear, discouragement, health issues, critically ill children, and being overweight… all of these in some way attacking my confidence. Cunningly and deceitfully, the devil is determined to crush courage
and cause fear, stealing, killing and destroying you. God defeated the devil
when the Father raised Jesus from the dead; so, let us put on God's armor,
confronting fear and standing firm in Jesus' resurrection power and vic-
tory. Let us challenge Satan's attacks, counterattacking with the sword of
the Spirit, God's word. (Ephesians 6:10-17)

Finally, only Jesus can give real inner courage and needed confidence
whether or not there is a human intermediary. In many and various ways,
the Lord will increase your confidence, encouraging, healing, compensat-

ing for your weaknesses, and providing needed training and experience so that you can live worthy of Jesus and His call. So, let's press on!

"For God did not give us a spirit of cowardice, but rather a spirit of power and of love and of self-discipline." 2 Timothy 1:7 NRSV

First Challenge: Increase Your Confidence

How has Jesus encouraged you, recently or in the past? How have other people given you inner courage? Think of specific instances.

_____

_____

_____

What builds and increases your confidence?

_____

_____

_____

What "steals, kills and destroys" your confidence?

_____

_____

_____

Every day, take note of how the Lord appears and encourages you. Keep a journal of these epiphanies. Picture and know that Jesus is with you right now:

"What then are we to say about these things? If God is for us, who is against us? He who did not withhold his own Son, but gave him up for all of us, will he not with him also give us everything else?" Romans 8:31 NRSV

Second Challenge: Give and Receive Healing

Your confidence can be injured, diminished and even destroyed by unhealed brokenness, hindering your ability to live in conformity with the Lord's call. Unhealed brokenness distracts, producing fear and hesitation. Brokenness can cause you to run from helpful feedback that is spoken in a positive manner (in contrast to words spoken without respect or harshly as an attack). Personal attacks hurt and harm. Unhealed brokenness can be transferred to other relationships, causing one to retreat inside, strike out, or be paralyzed. How is unhealed brokenness affecting or hindering you? How is it affecting your confidence?

_____

_____

_____

Practicing self-examination can heal and transform. Try this helpful exercise. Divide your life into three periods: childhood, adolescence and adulthood. Come before the Lord in prayerful reflection. With paper and pencil in hand, invite the Lord to reveal anything during your childhood that needs forgiveness, healing or both. Then wait in absolute silence for several minutes. Allow Jesus to gently whisper to you, revealing what is needed. Record all that comes to mind, not attempting to analyze any of it. On the next day, repeat the same exercise for your adolescence. On the third day, repeat it for your adult years. Next go to someone who understands confession, is non-judgmental, and utterly safe on confidentiality—perhaps someone you do not know. Honestly and specifically, reveal your reflections.[7]

_____

_____

_____

Seek out someone you have wounded— even if you hurt them long ago. Specifically and humbly acknowledge your offense. Ask for forgiveness. Quite likely, confessing your sin will free both of you from hurt, guilt and regret. Best of all, you both will be able to move unencumbered into the future. Who might be freed by your confession?

_____

_____

_____

Jesus gives wholeness through many safe and non-threatening means: healing prayer, anointing with oil, laying on of hands, encouragement, a medical doctor, a professional counselor, the passage of time, hearing Jesus speak, worship, and still more. Prayerfully reflecting upon the Lord's promises can also heal, transform, and help in persevering through hardship. Diminish difficulties by contemplating God's powerful promises. Use the list found in Appendix D. How is brokenness hindering or stealing your confidence? How will you seek wholeness? How will you persevere?

_____

_____

_____

The Lord is speaking to you:

"Are any among you suffering? They should pray. Are any cheerful? They should sing songs of praise. Are any among you sick? They should call for the elders of the church and have them pray over them, anointing them with oil in the name of the Lord. The prayer of faith will save the sick, and Lord will raise them up; and anyone who has committed sins will be forgiven. Therefore confess your sins to one another, and pray for one another, so that you may be healed. The prayer of the righteous is powerful and effective." James 5:13-16 NRSV

Third Challenge: Compensate for Your Weaknesses

Understanding others' gifts and how they can supplement and complement your own gifts will increase your effectiveness. Ironically, acknowledging and compensating for your weaknesses results in strength. What are your weaknesses? How do you need others' help? What spiritual gifts complement and supplement your own?

_____

_____

_____

God promises His strength and power to you:

"But God said to me, 'My grace is sufficient for you, for power is made perfect in weakness; So, I will boast all the more gladly of my weaknesses, so that the power of Christ may dwell in me.'" 2 Corinthians 12:9 NRSV

Fourth Challenge: Receive Training

Training increases confidence. Jesus trains and equips us, giving needed skills, experience and knowledge. Training frees from fear. Training enhances spiritual gifts, making them more effective. You can receive training through many means: Scripture, study, listening, spiritual disciplines, seminars, classes, workshops, problem solving, experience, mentors, coaches and colleagues. As you consider Jesus' call, what kind of training and equipping do you need? How could you address inadequacy? Who could help you? How could you gain experience?

_____

_____

_____

Spiritual depth is acquired through knowing and following Jesus. Spiritual depth enables more effective service. In addition to worship, Scripture, prayer and the ancient practices and traditions, study history. How could you acquire needed spiritual depth? Who could help you?

_____

_____

_____

God's word will train and equip you:

"All scripture is inspired by God and is useful for teaching, for reproof, for correction and for training in righteousness, so that everyone who belongs to God may be proficient, equipped for every good work." 2 Timothy 3:16-17 NRSV

Sometimes you may wonder why opportunities develop so slowly. Sometimes, the Lord still needs to equip and train, preparing you with needed insights, skills, abilities and experience.

Prayer: Prayerfully imagine and reflect upon the scene in Mark 7:31-37. Next picture Jesus praying and laying hands on each person in your family, taking them *"aside."* Sit in silence. Allow the Holy Spirit within you to give words for your prayers. Pray for the healing of brokenness in each of their lives. As you pray, *"look up to heaven"* and say: *"Be opened!"* Imagine each person being set free, *"loosed"* from pain and brokenness. Last, in like manner, imagine Jesus laying His healing hands upon you, setting you free and healing your brokenness.

Make a commitment to seek out someone to pray for you, laying hands upon you, anointing with oil and offering healing prayer on your behalf. Attend a worship service of healing, or go to a pastor, spiritual director or trustworthy friend.

Further Thoughts and Actions

- Study the companion volume, *Custom Designed: A Life Worthy of the Call*. For real life illustrations and to develop added insight, examine the corresponding chapter.

- **Each day, keep a journal of epiphanies.** Record how the living God appeared to you, encouraging you.

- **Continue to inventory your concerns and fears.** Inventory your insecurities, inadequacies or lack of confidence. Ask God to give revelation and wisdom.

- **Random Thoughts:** Record any thoughts, feelings, ideas or actions that come to you.

CHAPTER 12
CUSTOM DESIGNING A LIFE WORTHY OF THE CALL

The Lord is Calling: Matthew 7:21-27; Ephesians 3:20-4:1; Colossians 1:9-12; 3:12-17

Throughout the ages, Christians have established patterns of life, sometimes called "rules." A pattern of life is a custom designed blueprint or plan for your life. A pattern of life is helpful for integrating insights into your life's rhythm, and pressing on in developing a deep and profound friendship with Jesus, knowing, following and serving Him.

To create your pattern, prayerfully and intentionally choose practices and steps that will lead to fruitfulness, meaning, joy, balance and wholeness. A well-designed pattern of life should facilitate and encourage living in conformity with Jesus and His call. This is our hope and prayer:

"We continually ask God to fill you with the knowledge of his will through all the wisdom and understanding that the Spirit gives, so that you may live a life worthy of the Lord and please him in every way: bearing fruit in every good work, growing in the knowledge of God, being strengthened with all power according to his glorious might so that you may have great endurance and patience, and giving joyful thanks to the Father, who has qualified you to share in the inheritance of his holy people in the kingdom of light." Colossians 1:9b-12

Pattern of Life: Example 1

Call to Know Jesus

- I will spend five minutes with Jesus in the evening. I will reflect upon a verse or two of scripture.
- Until I find a church that fits me, I will worship at two different churches each month.

Call to Follow Jesus

- I will seek to find a Bible study so that I can deepen my knowledge of God's word. Weekly, I will attend this study.

Call to Serve Jesus

- When I travel on an airplane, I will set aside an hour to work on one of the sections in this guide.
- In the next six months, I will attend a class on spiritual gifts.
- I will serve food and do clean-up at church events.
- Twice a month on Friday night, I will have a date with my wife.
- At my job, I will consider what is energizing and fulfilling to me and what is not. I will invite God to give me wisdom in my work and how to demonstrate the gospel.
- In my spaces of time, I will reflect upon scriptural financial principles, and pray about how I can make needed changes.
- I will volunteer at the food pantry.

Pattern of Life: Example 2

Call to Know Jesus

- I will worship weekly, hearing God's word and celebrating the Lord's Supper. I will write one new insight that I learned from God's word. I will keep the Sabbath from Saturday evening to Sunday evening, ceasing, resting and worshipping.
- Daily with my first available time, I will spend fifteen minutes with Jesus. I will begin by resting in His love. I will pray the letter that I wrote to God. I will use a devotional from church for the remainder of the time.
- I will walk in the early evening on Tuesday and Friday evenings. While I walk, I will pay attention to my thoughts, listening for the Holy Spirit speaking to me.

Call to Follow Jesus

- Once a month I will set aside a Saturday morning for intentional time with Jesus. The first time, I will write a letter to God. As a part of this letter, I will invite the Holy Spirit to continually fill me. After this initial time, I will use my time for solitude and meditation on Scripture, trying new ways to practice spiritual disciplines.
- Once a month I will arrange to have an intentional conversation with a trustworthy friend. Before meeting, I will pray about what I might like to share.

Call to Serve Jesus

- Over the next six months, I will evaluate how I am presently serving. I will explore new opportunities that use my shepherding and intercession spiritual gifts.
- On Sunday afternoon, I will spend one half hour reflecting upon my uniqueness and how I might better use my unique attributes in all of life.
- Weekly I will look for new opportunities to give my resources.
- On Sunday afternoons once a month, I will spend one hour contemplating my mission field: my work, family and home, church, neighborhood, community and world.
- On my commute over the next three months, I will consider why I am restless at work.

Though these examples are written in narrative form, a few words will suffice. As you review these examples, you may be tempted to compare yourself or copy one of them. Resist this temptation. Remember your pattern of life should be custom designed for you. Establishing an intentional pattern of life will allow you to live more fully and intentionally in conformity with Jesus' call. Press on!

"And whatever you do, whether in word or deed, do it all in the name of the Lord Jesus, giving thanks to God the Father through him." Colossians 3:17

First Challenge: Custom Design a Pattern of Life

Record your pattern of life on the worksheet provided in Appendix F. As food for thought, review your reflections and the many time-tested ideas, disciplines and practices throughout this guide. If creating a pattern of life is new, begin by using the worksheet to record your present practice, and then use it to draft your intentions for the future. Jot down initial thoughts and ideas.

_____

_____

_____

In order for God to guide you, a pattern of life is best designed in the context of quiet, careful and prayerful reflection. If needed, ask someone with wisdom and experience to help you, perhaps your pastor or spiritual director or one of your trustworthy companions.

Choose spiritual practices that are desirable. Remember spiritual practices are not for earning the approval, favor or love of God or others. You have all of Jesus' love and favor now. What do you want to include in your pattern of life?

_____

_____

_____

As you custom design your own unique pattern of life, keep in mind some guidelines. Make your pattern flexible and simple, selecting a few helpful practices. Make sure your pattern feels comfortable. Be specific. Record when, where, how often, and how you will do the various practices. Think about what will work best for your unique situation. Design a pattern that is attainable, choosing practices that are realistic. Sections of the worksheet may be left blank for future growth or contemplation.

Regularly reevaluate your pattern, revising it as needed—perhaps every six months to a year or oftener—especially if your pattern is not working or becomes irrelevant as your life evolves and changes. Identify what isn't working and make needed changes. Be assured by these words:

"For everything there is a season, and a time for every matter under heaven: a time to be born, and a time to die; a time to plant, and a time to pluck up what is planted; a time to kill, and a time to heal; a time to break down, and a time to build up; a time to weep, and time to laugh; a time to mourn, and time to dance; a time to throw away stones, and a time to gather stones together; a time to embrace, and time to refrain from embracing; a time to seek, and a time to lose; a time to keep, and time to throw away; a time to tear, and time to sew; a time to keep silence, and time to speak; a time to love, and a time to hate; a time for war, and time for peace." Ecclesiastes 3:1-8 NRSV

Prayer: Talk to Jesus about your pattern of life. Express to Jesus your desire to know, follow and serve Him in all of life. Reflect upon this verse from Scripture:

"I urge you to live a life worthy of the calling you have received." Ephesians 4:1

Express to Jesus your desire to live worthy of Him and His call. Ask Jesus to give you specific guidance on needed steps to move ahead. Ask Jesus to give you wisdom on how to arrange your time, making those steps possible. Sit in silence for a few minutes. Pay attention to your thoughts. Thank Jesus for the insights and promptings He gives.

Further Thoughts and Actions

- **Study the companion volume, *Custom Designed: A Life Worthy of the Call*.** For real life illustrations and to develop added insight, examine the corresponding chapter.

- **Random Thoughts:** Record any thoughts, feelings, ideas or actions that come to you.

Practical Tools and Resources

Appendices and Endnotes

Appendix A

Talents, Skills and Abilities

Appendix B

Spiritual Gifts Inventory

Appendix C

Spiritual Gifts Descriptions

Appendix D

Diminishing Difficulties with God's Precious Promises

Appendix E

Take Steps

Appendix F

Pattern of Life Worksheet

Endnotes

Answer Sheet: Spiritual Gifts Inventory

APPENDIX A

TALENTS SKILLS AND ABILITIES CHECKLIST

Checklist of Talents Skills and Abilities

Performance Skills
____ Public Speaking
____ Presentations
____ Preaching
____ Lecturing
____ Comedy
____ Spontaneity
____ Dance
____ Dramatics:
   Skits & Plays
____ Dramatics:
   Speaking & Reading
____ Pantomime
____ Puppeteer
____ Singing: Solos & Duets
____ Choir
____ Small Group Singing
____ Musical Instrument
Specify:
____ Compose Music
____ Leading Games
____ Signing for the Deaf
____ Other... Specify:

Artistic & Creative Talents
____ Creating & Innovating
____ Drawing
____ Painting
____ Woodworking
____ Displays
____ Posters & Charts
____ Scrapbooks
____ Knitting
____ Crocheting
____ Stitchery
____ Sewing
____ Weaving & Banners
____ Photography
____ Making Videos
____ Graphic Arts
____ Web Design
____ Child Crafts
____ Adult Crafts
____ Decorating
____ Interior Design
____ Other... Specify:

Practical & Manual Skills
____ Masonry
____ Maintenance
____ Landscaping
____ Lawn Mowing
____ Trimming:
   Shrubs & Other
____ Gardening
____ Electrical
____ Plumbing
____ Mechanical
____ Small Engine Repair
____ Heating &
   Air Conditioning
____ Inventing
____ Engineering
Specify:
____ Computer Skills
____ Carpentry
____ Cabinet Making
____ Remodeling
____ Painting
____ Wallpapering
____ Cleaning
____ Cooking & Baking
____ Large Quantity Cooking
____ Organize Meals
____ Other... Specify:

People Skills & Talents
____ Welcoming
____ Talking with Strangers
____ Listening
____ Teaching
____ Tutoring
____ Training
____ Team Building
____ Motivating & Inspiring
____ Working with Groups
____ Recruiting
____ Mediating
____ Solving Conflicts
____ Troubleshooting
____ Foreign Language
Specify:
____ Other... Specify:

Business & Management
____ Data Entry
____ Filing
____ Record Keeping
____ Data Base
   Management
____ Web Page
   Management
____ Library Skills
____ Editing & Proofing
____ Reporting
____ Bookkeeping
____ Accounting
____ Financial
____ Budgeting
____ Receptionist
____ Telephoning
____ General Office
____ Administration
____ Organization
____ Coordination
____ Planning
____ Setting Priorities
____ Running Meetings
____ Making Policy
____ Other... Specify:

Writing Skills & Talents
____ Informational
____ News
____ Devotions
____ Essays
____ Stories
____ Drama
____ Poetry
____ Other... Specify:

Outreach Talents & Skills
____ Marketing &
   Promoting
____ Human Relations
____ Cultural Trends
____ Research &
   Demographics
____ Fundraising
____ Other... Specify:

For more skills and talents, see *What Color is Your Parachute?* By Robert Nelson

APPENDIX B

SPIRITUAL GIFTS INVENTORY

Dear Friends,

Discover how the Holy Spirit has empowered you! A thorough understanding of your spiritual gifts will show how you can best serve the Lord and transform the world in everyday life: family, work, community, world and the gathering of believers. An inventory is a **useful tool** for identifying **your unique combination of spiritual gifts**.

Perhaps you feel one or more of these normal emotions:

- **Discomfort**: You may wonder what the results will indicate.
- **Guilt**: You may wish your scores were higher, or that you had less low scores.
- **Inferiority**: You may wonder how your scores will compare with others.

Here is a bit of help for these feelings. First, remember these feelings are normal. Second, rest assured! Everyone has some of these spiritual gifts! No one has all or many of the gifts. Third, the inventory indicates potential spiritual gifts. The inventory is designed so that some of your scores will be higher, and some or even many will be lower. Fourth, your mix of gifts is unique; therefore, everyone's results will be different. All gifts are needed and all are equally important!

Discovering and understanding your spiritual gifts is a process, sometimes taking a few years. An inventory is a helpful indicator to begin and facilitate this process; however, the best way to confirm and clarify your spiritual gifts is to experiment and use them.

Relax and have FUN! Discovering your gifts is energizing and exciting!

P.S. A few extra words...

- **Resources for understanding your spiritual gifts** and how to use them are available on the Call Inc. website: www.callnc.org
- **Purchase a photocopying license** for a modest price at www.callinc.org
  1. Go to the "Store" page.
  2. With a license, you can make unlimited copies of this inventory for a single congregation.
- Others may download this inventory for personal use at www.callinc.org

SPIRITUAL GIFTS INVENTORY

<u>Instructions for Use</u>: Complete the instructions for Steps 1-6! Enjoy!

<u>Step 1:</u>

- Remove or copy the **Answer Sheet** found on the final page of this book.
- Complete **Part I** (Questions 1-78). For each statement, mark on the **Answer Sheet** to what extent it is true in your life.

  4 = **True, consistently**
  3 = **True, a lot of the time**
  2 = **True, occasionally**
  1 = **True, infrequently**
  0 = **Rarely true**

- **Be honest! Do not** do a lot of self-analysis. **Do not** feel guilty about lower numbers. **Do not** record what you feel your response

should be. Whether the numbers are low or high is not the most important consideration. Be honest and put your first reaction to the statement.

PART I: FUNCTIONAL GIFTS

1. I have a lot of compassion. Often through practical acts of kindness and care, I have reached out to those who are troubled, neglected, and/or unlovable.

2. Repeatedly, God has spoken through me a message directed toward a specific person, group or situation.

3. I have provided spiritual care, nurture, or guidance to others, (young and/or old)—either an individual or a group.

4. By speaking an appropriate word at the right time, I have encouraged, consoled or counseled those who are discouraged and burdened.

5. I give generously of my wealth and money to the Lord's work with joyfulness, and not out of a sense of compulsion.

6. I enjoy befriending and spending time with persons who may not believe, especially hoping that perhaps an opportunity might come to share with them the gospel message of Jesus Christ.

7. I enjoy bearing the responsibility for the success of some particular plan, event or project. I am energized when it comes to completion in an effective manner.

8. I have effectively communicated the teachings of the Christian faith as they are found in the Scriptures in a manner that helps others learn and understand.

9. I enjoy generating excitement among others about the goals or vision of a group and/or church gathering.

10. I am content to do the less noticed practical jobs because I know someone has to do them.

11. Others have told me that they quickly feel at ease with me, even when they didn't know me.

12. I pray a lot and I enjoy it.

13. I think about and would like to see the Gospel of Jesus Christ extended to all peoples and cultures in the world.

14. I have a deep sense of fulfillment when I can help and invest my time in someone that others are often unwilling to help.

15. Others have told me that oftentimes my words seem as if they are a timely and an important message from God.

16. Others (young and/or old) will seek me out for guidance, help or direction regarding their faith in God.

17. I feel fulfilled when I know that my support, care and words have helped to lift the feelings of another.

18. I realize the Lord's work needs financial resources, and I am deeply moved to meet those needs whenever I can.

19. I find it easy and enjoyable to talk about Jesus with those who may not believe and trust Him.

20. I have been able to coordinate the necessary people, ideas, activities and/or resources in order to complete a project, plan, event or program.

21. I spend time thinking about how I might present important lessons so that others (young and/or old), will learn, understand and apply them to their lives.

22. Others respect my opinion and look to me for direction when I am in a group, even when someone else may be in charge.

23. When I serve the Lord, I am dependable and don't need much praise or thanks.

24. I have a desire to meet and get to know new people.

25. On a regular basis, I pray for concerns, needs, events and persons, often for extended periods of time.

26. I can easily adapt to differences in culture, language, lifestyle and locale.

27. I enjoy helping to meet the needs (often times, physical needs) of those who are less fortunate or often forgotten by others.

28. I am burdened by sin and when God's law is ignored. I have a deep concern for the truth and God's reputation.

29. I help others with their faith by doing one or more of the following: praying with them, sharing the Scriptures with them, giving guidance, getting to know them, sharing my faith experience, encouraging them to be involved with other Christians, and/or by inviting them to worship.

30. When I know someone is going through difficult times, I am motivated to build up this person and to speak words that will provide support, care and healing.

31. I know that I can give generously and even beyond the tithe (10% of my income) because I am confident that God will provide for all my needs.

32. I have shared, easily and joyfully, the basic gospel message in such a way that others have come to know Jesus Christ, and share in a saving relationship with Him as a result.

33. Others have told me that they thought a project or program that I was coordinating was well organized and smoothly run.

34. Others have told me that I have helped them to understand a difficult concept, idea or principle.

35. In a course of events, I am able to positively influence, persuade and motivate others to move forward with a course of action or towards a goal.

36. I see the many smaller tasks in the church (or other group) that need to happen, and I am willing to do them even if they are trivial or simple.

37. If I had the appropriate amount of space, I would be content to have Christian workers or other persons stay in my home for a period of time.

38. Others come to me requesting my prayers for their concerns because they know that I will follow through and consistently pray for them.

39. I have effectively shared the Gospel message of Jesus Christ with those of another culture, race or nation.

40. When I see someone in need, I feel an urgency to do whatever I can to reach out and help.

41. I have an earnest desire to speak messages that God gives me that will bring change.

42. I am concerned that others (young and/or old) might grow in their relationship with God through Jesus Christ, and I want to do all I can to help and care for them.

43. I have a strong desire to strengthen and reassure people in their faith, family or life.

44. I am deeply motivated to give as much as I can to the Lord's work by doing one or more of the following: making as much money as I can; managing my resources well; living frugally; living simply with few possessions; investing my money wisely; voluntarily lowering my standard

of living; or foregoing a good-paying job in order to give a significant amount of my time to the Lord's work;.

45. As the Lord gives opportunity, I have an earnest desire to share my faith in Jesus with as many as I am able.

46. I have a desire to see the church's mission and ministry, or the activities of another group run smoothly and efficiently.

47. I spend a lot of time studying and learning new insights about the Lord, Scripture, faith and/or life so that I can help others to understand them also.

48. I am concerned about the direction of the church or another organization, and am anxious to help it to move forward in its mission and service.

49. I enjoy knowing that my doing the many "behind the scenes" tasks helps in the overall effectiveness of the Lord's work.

50. In my home, church gathering, and/or in other settings, I enjoy making others, even strangers, feel comfortable and "at home".

51. Though a lot of people don't know that I am praying, I feel an excitement about my praying, knowing that people, the church and even the world can and have been changed.

52. I have felt an attraction and desire to be a missionary or church worker in another culture or country.

53. I have a strong desire to help and spend time with one or more of the following: cast-offs, strangers, the homeless, prisoners, the poor, the

handicapped, the elderly, those who are suffering, widows, those with difficult family circumstances, the chemically dependent, those who are homebound, the lonely, those with emotional problems and/or those who have screwed up their lives.

54. God has used me to speak a message containing one or more of the following: rebuke, call for repentance, correction, comfort, encouragement, a call for change, a word about the future (which has later came true), and/or direction.

55. I particularly enjoy getting to know others (young and/or old) so that I might help them to grow spiritually, and know the Lord better.

56. Others come to me when they are discouraged and/or to share their problems.

57. I am excited and enjoy knowing that my financial resources make a real difference in making the Lord's work happen.

58. Others have told me that they have felt comfortable talking with me about the faith prior to their becoming believers.

59. I am able to formulate, direct, organize and carry out the necessary elements and steps in order to accomplish and fulfill goals.

60. I enjoy seeing others (young and/or old) come to a real understanding of Jesus and Jesus' ways through my communication and teaching.

61. Oftentimes, when I speak my opinion in a group, others seem to listen and affirm what I have to say to the group.

62. I desire to relieve others in the church or other groups of the routine and practical matters so that they can get other projects done.

63. I enjoy hosting guests (food, lodging, other needs) in such a way that they feel warmly welcomed.

64. When I see needs and burdens, I am drawn to pray. Often God shows me how to pray and even speaks to me in my prayers.

65. I enjoy learning about the Lord's work in other parts of the world.

66. Others recognize my desire and motivation to get to know and to help those who are troubled.

67. I have a strong desire and urgency to speak God's truth even when it is unpopular and others may not like what I have to say.

68. I want to encourage and care for others so that they might know the love of Jesus Christ more deeply, and they might be motivated to follow Jesus in all of life.

69. When I speak genuine and positive words to another person who may need to hear them, I feel uplifted and encouraged myself.

70. When I give of my financial resources, I don't expect recognition or anything in return, and often times I will give anonymously.

71. I get excited knowing that others have come to know Jesus Christ through my sharing of the Gospel message.

72. I am organized and manage well all of the details so that plans can become reality.

73. I have a strong desire to help others know and understand the Scriptures, and the truths that are contained in them.

74. I like to be in charge. Rather than following someone else's lead, it is easier for me to be the leader of a meeting or in a group.

75. I would rather have someone tell me what needs to be done than to be in charge.

76. I like creating an atmosphere in a gathering of people, or in my home, where others feel like they belong.

77. Because I know that God is listening and responding to my prayers, I have a strong desire to pray as much as I am able.

78. I have several friends who are from a different race, language or culture.

Step 2:

- Complete Part II (Questions 79-108).
- As with Part I, for each statement (except Questions 103-108), mark on the answer sheet to what extent it is true for you.
                4= **True, consistently**
                3= **True, a lot of the time**
                2= **True, occasionally**

$1 =$ **True, infrequently**

$0 =$ **Rarely true**

- Follow the specific instructions for Questions 103-108.

PART II: MANIFESTATIONAL GIFTS

79. I believe that I have received practical insight, direction and/or guidance from God for situations that are complicated or even problem-some.

80. The Holy Spirit has revealed to me information and insights that I did not learn through natural or human means.

81. I can tell when teaching, preaching or religious communication is not true to the Scriptures.

82. I am able to trust God in circumstances where others cannot, and where success cannot be guaranteed by human effort and means.

83. Many people view health and healing only from a natural and/or scientific point of view, focusing mostly upon the physical, but I believe that God is powerfully at work through prayer, medicine and other means ministering to the whole person.

84. God has worked through me to bring about supernatural signs and wonders that are largely unexplainable.

85. In groups, I believe that I often have a strong God-given sense of the appropriate action and/or direction where others don't have a sense of this at all.

86. I have suddenly known something about someone else that was accurate, but I did not know how I knew this.

87. I have accurately perceived phoniness or deceit in a person's character, sometimes based upon first impressions.

88. I get excited and can see God's vision for a group. Opposition or the lack of support from other people does not derail me.

89. When I lay hands on the sick and pray for them, I sometimes feel tingling, warmth or other sensations, and that healing actually occurred.

90. Working through my prayers, God has made the impossible, possible.

91. Others have indicated that my practical advice was just what was needed for a particular situation in their life and faith.

92. I have insight or just know something to be true and later find out that it is true.

93. Others affirm the reliability of my perceptions or evaluations regarding spiritual circumstances or communication.

94. I believe that God can do incredible and even impossible things, and I have seen God do these things in a tangible way.

95. I earnestly desire and enjoy praying for the sick and suffering, hoping that God may heal through me.

96. I have experienced God's power or intervention to do things that cannot be explained by natural explanations.

97. I believe that God enables and helps me to make appropriate application of Christian teaching to specific situations and problems.

98. Through my own reflection and study, I get excited when I believe that God has given me a sudden revelation and understanding of Christian teaching and principles.

99. God sometimes allows me to readily distinguish between spiritual truth and error, good and evil, right and wrong, or Satanic and godly.

100. When I sense that God is active and present in an undertaking or circumstance, I can move forward in spite of other people's pessimism.

101. Others have sought me out, and they have told me that God healed them of a physical problem when I prayed for them.

102. Others can confirm that God has used me to bring about visible miracles.

103. Have you ever spoken in tongues? Yes or No? If yes, skip to 105.

104. If No, do you have a desire to speak in tongues? Yes or No? Skip to 106.

105. If Yes, how frequently?
    4=frequently 3=fairly often 2=regularly 1=occasionally 0=seldom

106. Have you ever interpreted the public gift of tongues? Yes or No? If Yes, skip to 108.

107. If No, do you have the desire to interpret the public gift of tongues? Yes or No? Skip to Step 3.

108. If yes, how frequently?
4=frequently 3=fairly often 2=regularly 1=occasionally 0=seldom

Step 3:

- Complete **Part III** (Questions 109-132).
- For each statement, mark on the answer sheet to what extent it is true for you.

4 = **True, consistently**

3 = **True, a lot of the time**

2 = **True, occasionally**

1 = **True, infrequently**

0 = **Rarely true**

PART III: GIFTS OF EXPRESSION

109. I have expressed my Christian faith in music—vocal and/or instrumental.

110. I have a desire to express my Christian faith in music—vocal and/or instrumental.

111. Others comment that the Lord has used my message of faith expressed in music in their lives.

112. I get excited and energized when I know that the Lord's work has been furthered through my music—vocal and/or instrumental.

113. I have expressed my Christian faith through arts and crafts.

114. I have a desire to express my Christian faith through arts and crafts.

115. Others have commented that the Lord has used my faith message expressed through arts and crafts.

116. I get excited and energized when I know that the Lord's work has been furthered through something that I have designed or made.

117. I have expressed my Christian faith through one or more of the following expressions of speech: public speaking or preaching, monologue/dialogue, spontaneity or comedy.

118. I have a desire to express my Christian faith through one or more forms of speech.

119. Others comment that the Lord has used my spoken message of the faith in their lives.

120. I get excited and energized when I know that the Lord's work has been furthered through my speaking.

121. I have expressed my Christian faith through drama and/or dance.

122. I have a desire to express my Christian faith through acting, performing or dancing.

123. Others comment that they enjoy my acting or dancing, and that the Lord spoke to them through my acting or performing.

124. I get excited and energized when I know that the Lord's work has been furthered through my acting or dancing.

125. I have expressed my Christian faith in writing.

126. I have a desire to express my Christian faith in writing.

127. Others comment that the Lord has spoken to them through my writing.

128. I get excited and energized when I know that the Lord's work has been furthered through my writing.

129. I have a creative ability to use my hands to design, create, build and/or fix things that are useful in serving God.

130. I have a desire to express my faith in tangible, practical ways through the use of my hands.

131. Others appreciate my ability to serve the Lord and the church through my use of tools, machines and my hands.

132. I enjoy honoring God by using my hands to build, make or fix things that will be used in the Lord's work.

Step 4:

- Across each line on the **Answer Sheet**, total all the numerical entries and record in the "total" column.

- After totaling, continue with **Step 5** on the next page.

Step 5: Match the appropriate total from each line of the **Answer Sheet** with the gift bearing the same letter below. Transfer the totals from the **Answer Sheet** to this page.

Part I: FUNCTIONAL MOTIVATIONAL GIFTS

    A.   Mercy _____

    B.   Prophecy _____

    C.   Shepherding _____

    D.   Encouragement - Exhortation _____

    E.   Giving _____

    F.   Evangelist _____

    G.   Administration - Administrative Leadership _____

    H.   Teaching _____

    I.   Leadership _____

    J.   Service - Helps _____

    K.   Hospitality _____

Spirit Empowered Calls

    L.   Intercession _____

    M.   Missionary _____

Part II: MANIFESTATIONAL GIFTS

    A.   Wisdom _____

    B.   Knowledge _____

    C.   Discernment _____

    D.   Faith _____

    E.   Healing _____

    F.   Miracles _____

G.	Tongues	103. (Have done it) yes___no___
		104. (Desire) yes___no___
		105. (Frequency)_____
H.	Interpretation	106. (Have done it) yes___no___
		107. (Desire) yes___no___
		108. (Frequency)_____

Part III: GIFTS OF EXPRESSION

- A. Music _____
- B. Arts and Crafts _____
- C. Speech _____
- D. Drama/Dance _____
- E. Writing _____
- F. Manual Craftsmanship _____

Step 6: Use your gifts! You are called by Jesus and empowered by His Spirit with spiritual gifts in order to transform the world. For more spiritual gifts teaching, check out other Call Inc. resources at www.callinc.org including:

Custom Designed: A Life Worthy of the Call

We the Christian Church: "Called Out" by Jesus

APPENDIX C
SPIRITUAL GIFTS DESCRIPTIONS

Spiritual Gifts Descriptions

Jesus showed evidence of all the scriptural spiritual gifts except speaking in tongues. The Holy Spirit has equipped you with God's power, endowing you with the spiritual gifts that Jesus possessed. Quite naturally, they supernaturally motivate and create competence so that you can effectively live worthy of Jesus and His call, continuing His kingdom purposes and serving Him and others in everyday life. More so than anything else, your spiritual gifts will shape and form your call.

Each gift will be described by a simple list of characteristics, behaviors, motivations or purposes. As you study each gift, ask yourself: *"Is this a gift that God has given to me?" "Do I have the characteristics, behaviors and attributes of this gift?" "To which gifts am I drawn?" "Which of these do others see and affirm in me?"* Take note of characteristics you possess even if you use these characteristics differently than described.

Understanding these four spiritual gift categories will help you to know how your own gifts function.

- **"Functional" Gifts**
- **"Equipping" and Functional Gifts**
- **"Manifestational" Gifts**
- **Gifts of Expression.**

"Functional" Gifts (Romans 12:3-8 and 1 Corinthians 12:7-10): All of us together are the Body of Christ, each with a unique part and "function:"

"For as in one body we have many members, and not all the members have the same function … we have gifts that differ" Romans 12:4, 6b NRSV

Your combination of functional gifts will define how you "function" while serving the Lord. Functional gifts cause intense motivation, extraordinary effectiveness and a deep desire to pursue certain goals and activities. In my experience, people seem to have two to four functional gifts.

Service (Romans 12:7): People with this gift show their love for God and others by doing nuts and bolts tasks. "Nuts and bolts" tasks are behind the scenes small, but very necessary and defined tasks that like nuts and bolts, hold together an organization, event or project. For example, people with this gift may enjoy setting up or taking down an event, running errands, fixing equipment, maintaining a facility, or preparing and serving food.

Encouragement (Romans 12:8): People with this gift build up other people, giving them inner courage. Functioning as cheerleaders, they are genuinely positive. They notice when others are discouraged, often having the right word for a situation. The Biblical Greek word for this gift literally means "called-alongside."

Mercy (Romans 12:8): People with this gift have deep concern and compassion for people who are ostracized, disadvantaged or on the fringes of life. For example, people with this gift may have profound concern and compassion for one or more of these groups: the handicapped, elderly, poor, oppressed, homeless, addicted, prisoners, AIDS victims or those who have screwed up their lives. People with this gift may be easily moved to tears.

Administration or Administrative Leadership (1 Corinthians 12:28): People with this gift effectively coordinate all the necessary tasks, details, people and resources to execute and make something happen.

Words describing this gift are: organization, management, and detail-oriented. People with this gift may have a people-oriented focus, a task-oriented focus or both orientations. The Biblical Greek word for this gift means "governing leadership." Though often it is translated "administration," this gift is a leadership gift though different in nature from the other "leadership" gift.

Leadership (Romans 12:8): People with this gift have a God-given influence and authority with people. God-given implies that these people are able to influence quite naturally without control and emotionalism though at times they might manifest these tendencies. Often they think and operate ahead of others. They are big picture thinkers. The Biblical Greek word for this gift literally means "to stand in front."

Giving (Romans 12:8): People with this gift generously share their financial and material resources in order to meet kingdom needs. God inspires them to donate beyond the average committed Christian, often sacrificing and giving above the tithe. Though their giving is directed towards kingdom needs, it is not limited to a church gathering; instead, kingdom needs in various settings are supported. People with this gift have varying degrees of wealth… some with very modest means. One or more of the following may enable giving: earning a lot of money, wisely managing resources, foregoing a well-paying job to give time, being frugal, living simply, sacrificing, wisely investing, or voluntary austerity.

Hospitality (1 Peter 4:9-10, Romans 12:13): People with this gift are intensely motivated to love and welcome the stranger. They make outsiders feel safe, connected, comfortable, and at ease. The Biblical Greek word for hospitality literally means "love of the stranger." This gift may be expressed by directly interacting with people or by creating a welcoming atmosphere.

The next two gifts are not specifically named "spiritual gifts" in Scripture. They are specialized callings, operating like spiritual gifts.

Missionary (Acts 1:8, Matthew 28:18-20): People with this gift have a deep appreciation for other cultures. Sometimes they have a God-given openness to going anywhere, and a sense of adventure. Sometimes, they easily learn foreign languages.

Intercession (Luke 2:36-38): People with this gift are motivated beyond the average committed Christian to pray for extended periods of times. When their mental energy is not occupied, God will naturally turn their attention to praying about anything as led by the Holy Spirit.

"Equipping" and Functional Gifts (Ephesians 4:11): Equipping gifts prepare others for Jesus' transformative work, increasing their effectiveness.

"So Christ himself gave the apostles, the prophets, the evangelists, the pastors and teachers, to equip his people for works of service, so that the body of Christ may be built up until we all reach unity in the faith and in the knowledge of the Son of God and become mature, attaining to the whole measure of the fullness of Christ."
Ephesians 4:11-13

Shepherd (Pastor) (Ephesians 4:11): People with this gift are very relationship oriented. They spiritually nurture people through developing relationships. In Ezekiel 34, the Lord characterizes a true shepherd: seeking the lost; strengthening the weak; healing the sick; binding up the injured; and bringing back the strayed. Though the Biblical Greek word literally means "shepherd," often it gets translated "pastor," causing misunderstanding. This gift is not limited to those with a "pastor" title or role. Nor is the "pastor" title or role implied by the gift. In any church gathering, several will have this gift. As well, not all with a "pastor" role or title have this gift.

Teacher (Ephesians 4:11, Romans 12:7, 1 Corinthians 12:28): People with this gift spiritually present scriptural knowledge and wisdom, enlightening and training people. They enable kingdom insight (inner sight), causing people to be transformed. Often they are concerned about spiritual depth. Teachers are very motivated to learn.

Evangelist (Ephesians 4:11): People with this gift have a God-given effectiveness to communicate Jesus' gospel, resulting in conversion, repentance and trust in Jesus. Some evangelists preach while others use the gift in one-on-one interactions. Often when a church gathering grows rapidly, the primary preacher has an evangelist gift.

Prophet/Prophecy (Ephesians 4:11, Romans 12:6, 1 Corinthians 12:28): People with this gift have a deep concern for scriptural truth and authority, and as a result, ethics and morality. They are not afraid to speak when scriptural truth is at stake. They may be critical and abrasive. They often write or speak as a mouthpiece for God, receiving prophetic words on God's behalf (See "manifestational" gift of prophecy below).

Apostle (Ephesians 4:11, 1 Corinthians 12:28): People with this gift have extraordinary authority and influence that transforms leaders, people and culture. Commonly they exhibit characteristics of all the "equipping" gifts and miracles as well. Often they have a worldwide influence, and are highly respected by leaders of many Christian traditions. A person with an apostolic role such as a 'bishop" may not have this gift.

"Manifestational" Gifts: These gifts supernaturally "manifest" or make visible the Holy Spirit's power and kingdom purposes.

"To each is given the manifestation of the Spirit for the common good. To one there is given through the Spirit a message of wisdom, to another a message of knowledge by means of the same Spirit, to another faith by the same Spirit, to another gifts of healing by that one Spirit, to another miraculous powers, to another prophecy, to another distinguishing between spirits, to another speaking in different kinds of tongues, and to still another the interpretation of tongues." 1 Corinthians 12:7-10 NRSV

When these gifts operate, God's power, presence and glory are unmistakably evident and "manifest." People readily recognize the Holy Spirit's power and glory. All of these gifts have an unexplainable supernatural aspect.

"Manifestational" gifts supplement, complement and even correlate with the functional gifts. For example, people with a leadership gift may have frequent manifestations of wisdom or discernment. Those with a shepherd gift may have frequent manifestations of healing. Those with an intercession gift may have frequent manifestations of speaking in tongues.

Wisdom is supernatural insight inspired by the Holy Spirit to determine when, how and what to do or say in a specific situation or in general. (1 Corinthians 12:8)

Knowledge is the supernatural ability inspired by the Holy Spirit to see, know, or proclaim truth that could not be known except by divine revelation. Also, the Spirit may inspire the supernatural ability to master and rightly apply truth from God's word in an amazingly helpful way. (1 Corinthians 12:8)

Faith is supernatural vision inspired by the Holy Spirit to see and know what God is doing, and extraordinary belief that God will accomplish the impossible without tangible evidence to support its happening. This is different than using "faith" to speak of saving faith. Some people with frequent manifestations of this gift are visionaries, receiving a "vision" from God that may involve not only self but others. (1 Corinthians 12:9)

Healing is when the Spirit brings supernatural wholeness, using human prayer and action. "Supernatural" implies that Jesus works outside of medicine and the God-created natural healing processes. Jesus may also amplify medicine and the God-created natural healing process. (1 Corinthians 12:9)

Discernment is supernatural insight inspired by the Holy Spirit to sense and separate accurately whether a situation has its source in Satan, human flesh, the world, or God. (1 Corinthians 12:10)

Miracles occur when the Holy Spirit enables supernatural cause and effect, differing from the usual God-created cause and effect. Like with Jesus, a miracle's purpose is to bring glory to God, and blessing and faith to people. (1 Corinthians 12:10)

Prophecy is a direct message from God supernaturally inspired by the Spirit, spoken using a human pen or voice as a mouthpiece. Like the scriptural prophets, prophecy uses "first person" language. (1 Corinthians 12:10)

Tongues is prayer inspired by the Spirit, spoken in another language that has not been learned. This supernatural prayer language is spoken either to God, from God, or to offer praise to God. Tongues may be inaudible or audible. It is controllable by the one speaking. If audible to others, "tongues" needs the gift of interpretation. (1 Corinthians 12:10)

Interpretation of Tongues is supernatural translation inspired by the Holy Spirit of the "tongues" gift. (1 Corinthians 12:10)

Gifts of Expression are God-given talents empowered by the Holy Spirit for kingdom purposes. When the Holy Spirit fills you, then all your actions, talents, skills, and really everything can be empowered by the Holy Spirit causing them to operate like spiritual gifts.

"Then Moses said to the Israelites: See the LORD has called by name Bezalel... he has filled him with divine spirit, with skill, intelligence, and knowledge in every kind of craft, to devise artistic designs... And he has inspired him to teach, both him and Oholiab... He has filled them with skill to do every kind of work done by an artisan or by a designer." Exodus 35:30-32, 34a, 35a NRSV

Filled with the Holy Spirit, Bezalel and Oholiab created beautiful art for the tabernacle. Gifts of expression are found throughout Scripture, not just in the scriptural spiritual gift lists:

Music (Asaph, 1 Chronicles 25:1)
Arts and Crafts (Bezalel and Oholiab, Exodus 35:30-35)
Writing (Isaiah, Isaiah 1:1; 6:1-13)
Speech (Isaiah, Isaiah 61)
Drama (Song of Solomon)
Dance (David, 2 Samuel 5:3; 6:14)
Craftsmanship or Manual Crafts (Huram-abi, 2 Chronicles 2:13-14)

APPENDIX D

DIMINISHING DIFFICULTIES WITH GOD'S PRECIOUS PROMISES

Diminishing Difficulties With God's Precious Promises

God's precious promises will speak to you, sustaining you in the midst of the difficulties.

The D's: Difficulties

Darkness Disappointment Disillusionment Distraction Distress Despair Driven Doubt Danger Depression Discouragement Destruction Death

Diminishing the D's with the P's: God's Precious Promises

Pressing On: Philippians 3:7-14

Perseverance: Hebrews 12:1-3

Perspective: Romans 8:35-39

Play and Rest: Matthew 11:28-30

Prayer is a Conversation with God: Philippians 4:6-7

Possibility: Luke 1:37

Present Moment: Philippians 3:13; Matthew 6:34

Presence of God (all the time): Matthew 28:20; Hebrews 13:5-6

Peace and Wholeness: John 14:25-27; Philippians 4:8-9

Patience: Isaiah 40:30-31

Positives: 1 Peter 4:8, Romans 8:31

Partners: James 5:13-16

Preparation and Training: 1 Timothy 4:7-8

Practice: Matthew 7:24-27

Priorities: Matthew 6:33

Plan of God: Jeremiah 29:11-14

Purpose: 1 Corinthians 2:9

Power: 2 Corinthians 12:9; Ephesians 3:20-21

Praise: Ephesians 1:9

Pattern for Living: Ephesians 4:1

APPENDIX E

TAKE STEPS

Take Steps and Press On!

*"I want to know Christ and the power of his resurrection… Not that I have already obtained this or have already reached the goal; but I **press on** to make it my own… I **press on** toward the goal for the prize of the heavenly call of God in Christ Jesus." Philippians 3:10, 12, 14 NRSV*

"Press on" is race language. If you wanted to win an Olympic race, what would you need to do? If you want to win the prize of God's heavenly "call," … what do you need to do? Here are some suggestions to increase your effectiveness. Choose a couple of steps and "**press on!**"

T **Time & Money:** Jesus told a parable: *"It will be like a man going on a journey who called his servants and entrusted his property to them."* Matthew 25:14 (Author's translation) Either the Lord's call will determine the use of your time and resources, or poor time and resource spending choices will detour from His call. For help, see Chapter 10.

A **Ask for Help:** *"Without consultation, plans are frustrated, but with many counselors they succeed."* Proverbs 15:22 (NASB) Asking for help is a sign of strength. At times, everyone needs confidence, encouragement, or healing for hurts and regrets. See Chapters 7 and 11.

K **Know Follow Serve Jesus:** *"Calling the Twelve to him, Jesus began to send them out…"* Mark 6:7 Make it your #1 priority to know Jesus, and you will gain His kingdom perspective and participate in His kingdom purposes. See Chapters 5 & 6.

E **Equipped:** *"All Scripture…is useful for teaching…training in righteousness, so that the servant of God may be…equipped…"* 2 Timothy 3:16-17 Seek many opportunities to be equipped by God's word, a mentor, experience, or training. See Chapter 11, Challenge 4.

S **Stop & Listen:** *"Cease striving and know that I am God."* Psalm 46:10a (NASB) Cease, ask God for help, and learn to recognize the Lord's voice so that you can listen for His call and guidance. See Chapter 6.

T **Team:** *"And let us consider how we may spur one another on toward love and good deeds…"* Hebrews 10:24 Gather companions to support, pray, and keep you on track. Regularly connect with them, listening to their wisdom. See Chapter 7.

E **Eliminate Excuses:** Jesus told a parable: *"A certain man…preparing a great banquet…called many guests. But they all alike began to make excuses."* Luke 14:16-18 (Author's translation) Eliminate fear, misplaced priorities, sin (God abandonment), and love of money and possessions. Don't get fooled by the evil one! See Chapters 1, 9, 10 and 11.

P **Plan:** *"…walk in conformity with the calling to which you were called."* Ephesians 4:1 (Author's translation) Press on with Jesus' power to participate in His purposes. Live worthy of Jesus' call in the places of your unique mission field! See Chapters 9 and 12.

S **Surrender & Spirit:** *"Commit your way to the Lord, trust in him, and he will do this."* Psalm 37:5 Surrender control to the Lord! Follow Jesus! Welcome the Holy Spirit and His power into your life! See Chapter 9.

APPENDIX F

PATTERN OF LIFE WORKSHEET

Pattern of Life Worksheet

Call to Know Jesus

How will you deepen and grow your friendship with Jesus?

Record and describe practices that you will do. Be specific about how and when you will do them. Use words and phrases that will be easily remembered.

Call to Follow Jesus

How will you seek Jesus' guidance, following Him in all of life?

Record and describe practices that you will do. Be specific about how and when you will do them. Again use words and phrases that will be easily remembered.

Call to Serve Jesus

How will you serve Jesus in your unique mission field of life?

Describe opportunities, responsibilities and practices that you will do. Be specific. Incorporate these considerations:

- Use of your time
- Use of your spiritual gifts, talents, skills, knowledge, and experience
- Use of your money, home, material goods and property
- Witness: Sharing your experience of Jesus with others

Family and Friends

Work (career, volunteer, at home, school)

People of God... Church Gathering

Community/Neighborhood/World

Obstacles? What training and knowledge do you need (spiritual, practical, relationships, intellectual)? How and when will you obtain it? Who do you trust to give needed feedback and guidance?

Endnotes

[1] Bill Hybels, et. al., *"Imagine a Church"* video from *"**Network**,"* (Grand Rapids, MI: Zondervan, 1994)

[2] *Lutheran Book of Worship* (Minneapolis, MN: Augsburg Publishing & Board of Publication, Lutheran Church in America, 1978) p. 201.

[3] Richard Foster, *Celebration of Discipline,"* (New York, NY: Harper & Row, 1978) p. 131.

[4] Richard Foster, *"Prayer: Finding the Heart's True Home,"* (New York, NY: HarperCollins, 1992) p. 123.

[5] Rev. William Vaswig, *July 3, 1999* address at *"The Divine Conspiracy: A Renovare International Conference on Spiritual Renewal,"* June 30-July 3, 1999, Houston, TX.

[6] *Lutheran Book of Worship* (Minneapolis, MN: Augsburg Publishing & Board of Publication, Lutheran Church in America, 1978) p. 108.

[7] Richard Foster, *Celebration of Discipline,"* (New York, NY: Harper & Row, 1978) p. 131.

Answer Sheet: Spiritual Gifts Inventory

4= True, consistently 3= True, a lot of the time 2= True, occasionally
1= True, infrequently 0= Rarely true

Line		PART I: FUNCTIONAL GIFTS					TOTAL	Line
A.	1.___	14.___	27.___	40.___	53.___	66.___	_____	A.
B.	2.___	15.___	28.___	41.___	54.___	67.___	_____	B.
C.	3.___	16.___	29.___	42.___	55.___	68.___	_____	C.
D.	4.___	17.___	30.___	43.___	56.___	69.___	_____	D.
E.	5.___	18.___	31.___	44.___	57.___	70.___	_____	E.
F.	6.___	19.___	32.___	45.___	58.___	71.___	_____	F.
G.	7.___	20.___	33.___	46.___	59.___	72.___	_____	G.
H.	8.___	21.___	34.___	47.___	60.___	73.___	_____	H.
I.	9.___	22.___	35.___	48.___	61.___	74.___	_____	I.
J.	10.___	23.___	36.___	49.___	62.___	75.___	_____	J.
K.	11.___	24.___	37.___	50.___	63.___	76.___	_____	K.
L.	12.___	25.___	38.___	51.___	64.___	77.___	_____	L.
M.	13.___	26.___	39.___	52.___	65.___	78.___	_____	M.

PART II: MANIFESTATIONAL GIFTS

Line					TOTAL	Line
A.	79.___	85.___	91.___	97.___	_____	A.
B.	80.___	86.___	92.___	98.___	_____	B.
C.	81.___	87.___	93.___	99.___	_____	C.
D.	82.___	88.___	94.___	100.___	_____	D.
E.	83.___	89.___	95.___	101.___	_____	E.
F.	84.___	90.___	96.___	102.___	_____	F.
G.	103. yes___ no___ 104. yes___ no___					G.

105.____   ____   G.
H.   106. yes____ no____ 107. yes____ no____
          108.____   ____   H.

PART III: GIFTS OF EXPRESSION

Note: The numbers corresponding to the questions now go *across rather than down*.

A.   109.____ 110.____ 111.____ 112.____   ____   A.
B.   113.____ 114.____ 115.____ 116.____   ____   B.
C.   117.____ 118.____ 119.____ 120.____   ____   C.
D.   121.____ 122.____ 123.____ 124.____   ____   D.
E.   125.____ 126.____ 127.____ 128.____   ____   E.
F.   129.____ 130.____ 131.____ 132.____   ____   F.

AFTER TOTALING:

NOW complete Step 5 on the final page of the inventory.

7623846R00120

Made in the USA
San Bernardino, CA
13 January 2014